kids' crafternoon
sewing

kids' crafternoon
sewing

25 projects for a crafty afternoon

edited by Kathreen Ricketson

hardie grant books
MELBOURNE · LONDON

Contents

introduction **6**

sewing basics **8**

tools and materials **12**

safety **19**

fashion and style **20**

play and party **54**

read and relax **76**

spruce your space **110**

Introduction

Do you get a thrill from making things yourself? Are you the sort of person who likes nothing better than to rummage for some fabric and create something spontaneous and cool? Or do you plan ahead, prepare your materials, use a pattern and spend the day perfecting your design? Whatever your creative style, you will find lots to inspire you in this book. There are 25 uber-cool projects to make – all using fabric and sewing as the main material and technique. Some of the projects are quick to make, while others might take a bit longer, but the process of making and experimentation is all part of the creative buzz.

Use your imagination

How incredible is it to be able to make something for your room, yourself or your friends, just by using your imagination, some fabric and your sewing skills? You can up-end the scrap fabric bin and then spend the afternoon inventing doll designs, or you could grab a treasured fabric and make yourself a bag or a purse. Alternatively, you could recycle some old clothes to make highly original pillows for your bed. You might feel inspired to make a patchwork scarf, a monster reading pillow or even get creative with some embroidery. All the projects in this book are easy to customise, so you can mix and match once you get the hang of the techniques. If you like the concept but want to test out your own designs, or experiment with different materials from your scrap box, then go for it!

Get crafty

If you are new to sewing then spend some time reading the techniques section and practising on the sewing machine before starting. If you are already a fairly confident sewer then you can get stuck in straight away. Some projects may be a little more challenging than others and take more time and patience, but the extra effort will be worth it! Whatever your skill level you will find something to make in this book. Take your time to read through the instructions and gather your supplies before starting. Remember to stay calm, take plenty of breaks and ask for help if you need it. Don't worry if your project is not perfect. The most important thing is that you made it yourself and had a great time doing it! So plug in your iPod, grab a plate of shortbreads, some fresh homemade lemonade, and go and fossick in the fabric bin – then get sewing!

Sewing Basics

SETTING UP YOUR SEWING MACHINE

- Fill a few bobbins with the thread that you are using, so you don't have to stop and start in the middle of a project.
- Make sure that you have a good desk light and that your seat is comfortable – you don't want to strain your eyes or back!
- Check that you have a spare sewing machine needle or two. It's very annoying to have your last needle break while you are in the middle of a project. Most sewing machines require regular universal needles – change the needle before each new major project to get the best results.
- Check the tension on your stitches by doing a sewing test on a bit of scrap fabric. The upper and lower tensions must be balanced to produce a perfect stitch on both sides. Refer to the user manual if you need to change the tension.
- Keep your pins and pincushion near your sewing machine. A small pair of scissors to snip threads and a seam ripper/unpicker is essential.
- Thread your sewing machine with a neutral coloured thread, like grey or cream, or use the same colour as your fabric and fill your bobbin with the same colour thread.
- Set your sewing machine to a straight stitch and use a medium length stitch (approximately 3 mm).

BASIC SEWING TIPS

- When you pin your fabric pieces together, make sure that the good side of the fabric, called the 'right side' throughout this book, is on the inside, and the seams are on the 'wrong side'. When pinning, your pins should be at right angles to your fabric edge with the pin's head facing outward, this will make it much easier to remove your pins while you are sewing.
- Your seam allowance is the amount of space between the stitch line and the edge of the fabric. It should be about 1 cm. Use the edge of your sewing machine foot or the lines on the throat plate of your sewing machine as a guide to keep your seams straight.
- When sewing your seam, be sure to remove the pins as you come to them – if you sew over a pin you could break your needle.
- When sewing your straight line be sure to backstitch at the beginning and end to ensure your stitches don't come undone.

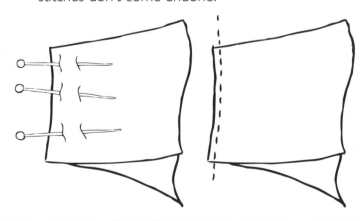

PREPARATION

Preparing your fabric. Wash and iron your fabric first – this is especially important if you are using recycled materials or dark colours like red and purple, as these colours could run the first time you wash them.

Tracing and cutting out patterns. Trace your patterns onto tracing paper or craft paper, then store these in a folder to re-use later.

Quick checklist
Gather all your materials, tools and supplies. Trace and cut out your pattern, wash and prepare your fabric, set up your sewing machine, check the lighting and your chair for comfort.

BASIC SEWING TECHNIQUES
Hand stitches
Running stitch. This is the simplest and most commonly used hand stitch. Pass the needle in and out of the fabric, keeping the length and the space of the stitches the same each time.

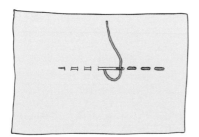

Whipstitch. This is a very basic over-and-over stitch that is used for joining. Insert the needle into the fabric at the same angle each time.

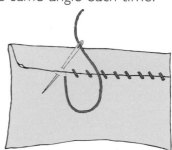

Backstitch. This stitch is very useful for drawing with thread. Take a backward stitch then bring the needle through in front of the first stitch.

Blanket stitch. This stitch is used on edges. This stitch is done from left to right. Insert the needle in the upper line and stitch straight down, keeping the thread under the point of the needle. Pull up the stitch to form a loop, and repeat.

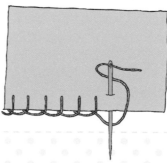

Cross stitch. This is probably the most widely used embroidery stitch – it forms a simple cross shape. Make your first stitch on a diagonal and then the second stitch is crossed over the top.

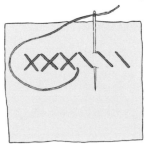

SEWING A BUTTON

1. Thread the needle with about 60 cm of thread then fold the thread in half and put a small knot in the end where both ends come together.
2. Place your button in position, and from the wrong side of the fabric, poke the needle and thread up through the fabric and into one of the buttonholes.
3. Place a pin on top of the button, and stitch over this when putting your needle back through the other buttonhole and through the fabric. This pin will stop your button from being too tightly secured to your fabric. Keep the pin there until you have finished sewing your button.

4. Repeat this process of pushing the needle through all the buttonholes in equal rotation, four or five times until the button is secure.
5. Push the needle out through the last buttonhole underneath the button but not through to the back of the fabric. Remove the pin and pull the button up to create a bit of slack under the button, wrap your thread around the stitches about six times and then push your needle through to the back of the fabric and knot the thread ends to secure the button.

SEWING A BASIC SHAPE

When sewing a cushion, pillow or stuffed toy, you will first need to sew a basic shape and then turn it right side out, stuff it and then sew up the gap. Here are some steps to help you with this process.

1. Cut out your basic shape: it could be a simple square or circle, or a trickier shape like the Cloudy Day Pillow on page 78 or Pet Pillow on page 86.
2. Pin your fabric together with the right sides facing each other on the inside and then sew all around the perimeter.
3. Leave a 10–15 cm gap unsewn on one side.
4. Remove all the pins then trim your seams if they have turned out too wide.
5. If you have curved bits, cutting small notches in the curved bits will help to ease the fabric around the curves when you are turning it inside out.
6. If you have corners, like in a square, then before turning them inside out, fold the seams down on each side of the corner and then poke them through using a chopstick (a pencil or wooden spoon handle can also be used).

7. Once your object is right side out, use your iron to press the seams all around, which will give your project a perfect finish.
8. Stuff your item using pillow stuffing. You can stuff it lightly or heavily depending on how firm or soft you want it to end up.
9. Whipstitch the gap closed by hand, using a needle and thread.

MAKING A FRENCH SEAM

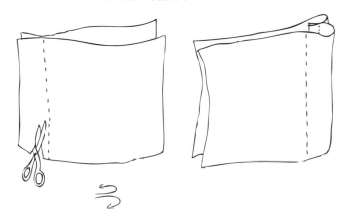

A French seam may sound fancy, but really isn't difficult. It is an easy way to get really sturdy and neat seams. French seams are especially good for bags, and you will use this technique on the Not Just a Bag project on page 50. A French seam assures a perfect finishing both on the inside and the outside and makes the seam of your project extra-sturdy.

1. Begin by pinning your fabric the opposite way you would normally. Pin with the wrong sides together and sew. Trim your seam allowance to 0.5 cm wide.

2. Turn the bag inside out, press your seams with an iron and pin, and stitch the side seams once more, this time giving your seams a wider seam allowance – about 1.5 cm seam allowance should do it. The first seam will be tucked inside the second one, which makes for an extra strong and perfectly finished seam.

FELTING A WOOL SWEATER

Don't throw out your felted wool jumpers – you can use them to make all sorts of things, including the iPod Creature Cosy on page 82. If you don't have any felted wool jumpers lying around you can felt some using old unwanted wool jumpers.

1. The sweater must be 100 per cent wool (the thicker the knit of the sweater, the heavier your finished fabric will be).
2. Wash your sweater in the washing machine, switched to the heavy-duty setting and using warm water with a small amount of washing-up detergent (a short squirt will do).
3. When the wash cycle is done, check to see if the sweater is felted to your liking – the wool knit should have thickened, and will likely be fuzzier and shrunken in size. It can take one to three washings to felt a wool sweater properly. Try washing jeans at the same time. Check the sweater after each washing since sweaters can felt at differing rates and once they felt, they can continue to felt further and shrink in size with each subsequent washing.
4. You can either air-dry or tumble-dry the felted sweaters.

Tools and Materials

MATERIALS

You can find lots of different kinds of fabric to use for your sewing projects just by searching around the house, before heading out to your local craft or second-hand store. Most of the projects in this book don't involve specialised tools or any fancy equipment, except for a sewing machine, so you will most likely find everything you need right at home. Even if you don't have access to a sewing machine, you can still make most of these projects by hand – they may just take a little bit longer.

Fabric

There are many fabrics to consider when you start sewing. They can be divided into two basic fibre categories: man-made fibres and natural fibres.

Man-made fibres. Polyester, nylon and acrylic are fabrics made from man-made fibres. They can be difficult to work with, but you may still be keen to experiment with some rather tricky fabrics like satin or fake fur.

Natural fibres. Wool, linen and cotton are fabrics made from natural fibres. They are the best fabrics as they are easy to work with and simple to care for, and they feel great. The majority of projects in this book incorporate natural fibres.

Then there are the different types of fabrics, including woven fabrics, knitted fabrics and novelty fabrics.

Woven fabrics and knitted fabrics. Woven fabrics, like calico, are easy to sew, they don't stretch out of shape and can be cut easily. These are the most common type of fabrics used for these projects. Knit fabrics, like T-shirt fabric, stretch a lot, so you won't be using them much with these projects, except maybe with the sassy sock softy.

Novelty fabrics. There are many kinds of novelty fabrics, like fake fur and felted wool. They can be tricky to sew but experimenting with them can be a lot of fun.

Start putting together a stash of fabrics you can use for the projects in this book. You don't need to spend a lot of money. Start by finding or recycling fabrics from your own house and then purchase your basic fabrics and some specialty fabrics.

Recycled fabrics. You can recycle fabric from all sorts of sources. Search around the house (or head to a second-hand shop) for souvenir linen teatowels, vintage tablecloths and pillowcases, shirts and skirts with nice fabric, T-shirts or sweaters, and even shopping bags. You can also recycle buttons, lace and trims from old clothing too!

Buying fabrics. When you need to go to a craft supply store to get in a few basic supplies, look for woven cotton fabric as it is really easy to cut and sew and washes well too. You might like to get calico, or plain coloured cottons, which are usually fairly cheap, but remember to look on the specials table for funky fabrics in fancy designs.

Buying specialty fabrics. If you do happen to go to a specialty fabric or quilting fabric shop, then you might be overwhelmed by the choice and variety of gorgeous fabrics. Instead of using up all your pocket money on lots of expensive materials, choose just a few pre-cut squares of designer fabrics to complement your other supplies. Other specialty fabrics like fake fur, inkjet-printable fabric and wool felt can be found at large craft stores.

Other supplies
As well as fabric, you will need thread and other materials for these sewing projects. Again, many items can be readily found around the home and through recycling, or at a craft or sewing supply store.

Threads. You will need some regular cotton or polyester sewing machine thread for your sewing machine. Don't buy the super-cheap stuff as it can break easily and wreck your machine. You will also need some embroidery threads – these are heavier threads than sewing machine thread and are used with a hand-sewing needle to decorate and embellish items.

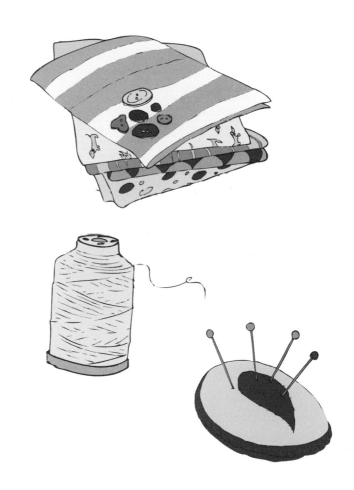

Pillow stuffing. You will need to have some stuffing on hand to fill your pillows and dolls – and monsters – when you make them. Recycle old pillows and use their stuffing again, or you can purchase polyester fibrefill or natural fibre toy filling from craft stores.

Freezer paper and fusible (iron-on) interfacing. Both these specialty materials are often used in sewing and they can be found in craft or sewing stores.

- Freezer paper comes in a roll and is great for making stencils or temporarily stabilising fabric. You will use it in the Pet Pillow project on page 86. It has a smooth, waxy side that can be temporarily stuck onto your fabric (with a hot iron) and then easily peeled away.
- Fusible (iron-on) interfacing is a bit like stiff fabric with one sticky side. You iron it onto the wrong side of your material and it adheres permanently (see the How to Use box opposite). Interfacing stiffens your material, which is useful for projects like the Mushroom Brooch on page 22.

Using fusible (iron-on) interfacing

Fusible interfacing (also known as fusible webbing, iron-on interfacing or Vilene) can be found in any craft or fabric shop. There are different thicknesses of interfacing for various projects, and the iron-on varieties have either single- or double-sided adhesive. For the projects in this book you will need a medium weight single-sided fusible interfacing. If you are unsure about the type to buy, ask for assistance.

The fusible interfacing makes a permanent bond, and it is important to get it right the first time, because after you have set the fusible interfacing, there's no undoing it. You might want to test a scrap on your fabric first before doing the whole piece. Be sure to read the manufacturer's directions before starting.

How to use

1. Place your fabric on your ironing board wrong side up. Centre your fusible interfacing on top of it, adhesive side down (the adhesive side is slightly rough).
2. Set your iron on a medium heat with the steam setting on.
3. Press your hot iron onto your interfacing and use downward pressure for about 15 seconds. When moving your iron to another section, lift it – rather than slide it – and then press. Leave the interfacing to cool for a minute before checking if it has adhered; if not, repeat this process.
4. Leave your fabric in place until it has cooled completely before touching it.

Elastic. This super stretchy band comes in different widths, thicknesses and strengths and has all sorts of uses. You will need some thin elastic for the Notebook Cover on page 90.

Extras. Ricrac, ribbons, buttons, wire, craft magnets, velcro, brooch backs, safety pins, craft glue and elastic, these extras are all pretty self-explanatory. They can be found at craft stores or even your local supermarket. See the projects for specifics about each of these materials.

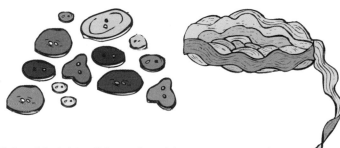

Printable inkjet fabric. Anything you can print on paper, you can print on fabric. All you need is an inkjet printer, a digital image and your inkjet fabric sheet. You can buy inkjet fabric sheets at a stationery store, or you can iron freezer paper onto your fabric to stabilise it to go into your printer – see the Pet Pillow project on page 86 to find out how.

Plastic canvas. is a lightweight plastic gridded material that is used to create 3D stitch designs. You can find this at craft or sewing shops and you will use it to create the Jellyfish Pendant on page 30.

TOOLS

You don't need much equipment for the projects in this book; just a few basic sewing tools should do the trick. A threaded sewing machine is essential, and with a ruler and scissors you are set to go. Of course you might want a few extra gadgets to help you along the sewing path.

Sewing machine

You will need a sewing machine for many of the projects in this book. It doesn't have to be fancy; a simple second-hand sewing machine will do, as long as it can do straight stitch and maybe zigzag.

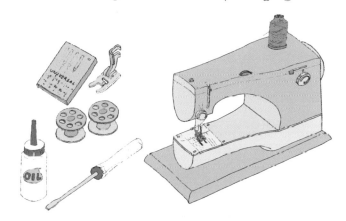

It is important to care for your machine. Take it for a regular service and learn how to clean it properly. Use the machine's manual and small toolkit (usually a small screwdriver, lint brush, sewing machine oil and tweezers) to maintain it and learn how to thread your machine.

Your sewing machine will come with a presser foot and a throat plate with markings on it. Use these to guide your seam allowance when sewing, and to help keep your seams straight. The bobbin is the small spool of thread underneath your throat plate; you will need to refill this when it runs out. Use the same thread as you are using at the top.

BASIC SEWING TOOLS

Iron. You will use an iron to press your seams and your final project. Remember to press, not glide, to prevent any stretching of fabric. Use an ironing board or lay out a towel onto your table. Be sure to keep your iron away from younger people and keep the cord away from tripping feet. When you are finished switch off and unplug the iron. When it has cooled down put the iron away in a safe spot.

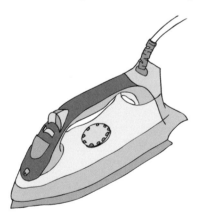

Scissors. You will need three basic types of scissors: small, sharp scissors for clipping seams and snipping threads; a really good pair of fabric scissors that you should use for fabric only (as using them on paper will dull the blade); and a pair of general scissors, for cutting paper. You may also find it useful to have pinking shears and decorative-edged scissors.

Tape measure and ruler. You will need a good, wide ruler and a tape measure. The ruler is handy for drawing and cutting straight lines and the tape measure is good for measuring around curves, objects and people.

Hand-sewing needle and thread. When you are hand-sewing, whether it is just to close up the gap in your pillow or toy where you put the stuffing in, or a bigger sewing project like the Sweet Embroidered Bird on page 120, you will need a hand-sewing needle and thread.

Embroidery hoop and thimble. An embroidery hoop holds your fabric at an even tension while you hand-sew. Place your fabric in between the rings and tighten with the screw. A thimble will protect your finger while you are hand-sewing.

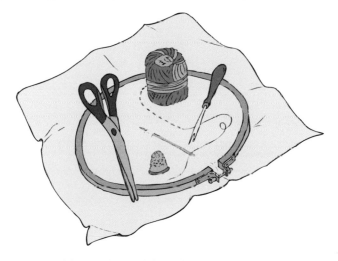

Chopstick. Use a chopstick to help turn legs right side out and push stuffing deep down into legs. You can also use a pencil or the handle of a wooden spoon.

SPECIALTY TOOLS FOR CRAFT PROJECTS

Iron-on transfer pencils and carbon paper. When tracing your embroidery designs onto fabrics, first use a transfer pencil to trace the design in reverse onto regular paper, then flip the paper over and iron the design onto your fabric. You can use dressmaker's carbon paper to do this. Buy transfer pencils and dressmaker's carbon paper at a craft store. Use tracing paper or plain brown craft paper to trace your templates.

Bias tape maker. If you wish to make your own binding strips, you can use this gadget. You feed strips of fabric in one end and as the fabric comes out folded through the other end you press it with a hot iron so it holds its shape. You can find these at most fabric and craft stores. Check how wide to cut your fabric; each tape-making gadget is different, so read the instructions on yours before cutting your fabric.

DIY bias tape. If you don't have a tape maker, you can still make your own binding tape at home. First cut strips of fabric about 6 cm wide and as long as you need. Sew strips together to get extra long pieces. Using a hot iron, press the strip of fabric all the way down the centre lengthways. Open it up and fold each side into the centre fold and press again. This is a bit of a long process but you will end up with lovely handmade binding tape that will coordinate perfectly with your projects. Use this tape to make the Bunting Flags on page 116.

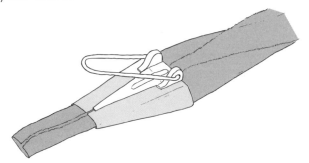

SAFETY

Using a sewing machine and crafting tools requires some basic common sense and safe handling. Don't leave tools lying around – always put them away after you have finished with them. Here are a few more specific safety tips:

A sewing machine has a sharp needle going up and down very quickly, so it is important to keep your fingers away from the needle while it is moving.
- Use controlled movements while the machine is running and avoid placing your fingers in front of the needle; instead, guide your object from the side of the needle's path
- Don't look away from the machine while it is running.

An iron can cause burn injuries if you are not careful.
- Iron on a high, stable surface such as an ironing board or table. Don't use the iron on the floor.
- Make sure the electrical cord is out of reach of younger people and is not a tripping hazard.
- Unplug the iron immediately after use. Remember, the iron can take a while to cool down after it is turned off.

Scissors have sharp tips and blades, so you need to be careful to put them away when they are not in use.
- Don't walk around carrying scissors or wave them around while talking.
- Watch where you are cutting, and keep your fingers out of the way.
- Store your scissors in a safe place out of reach.

A craft knife (sometimes called a utility, Stanley or X-ACTO knife) is potentially dangerous to use and requires care and consideration.
- Always remember to retract the blade and replace the safety sleeve after use, and keep the knife in a secure place when not in use.
- Use with a metal ruler and avoid placing your free hand too close to the blade.
- Use slow movements when cutting.
- Point the blade's cutting edge away from your body, and never cut toward the fingers or the hand that is holding the paper.
- It is not necessary to sharpen the blade. Instead, you will need to occasionally replace the old blade with a new one – take care to dispose of the old blade properly.

An awl is a very sharp needle used to poke holes through thick card, leather or layers of paper – always treat it with care.
- Don't leave your awl around for people to play with. Always replace it in its safety sleeve when you are finished with it.
- Always watch where you are poking it. Be careful to protect your table and your hands when you are using it.

Acrylic paints, glitter paints, and glue: there are many types of glues and paints available, so be sure to choose non-toxic and water-based paints and glues for your projects.
- Protect your work surface with newspaper and wear protective clothing such as a plastic apron or old shirt.
- If you do spill paint or glue unexpectedly, clean it up immediately with a warm damp cloth.
- Always clean the nozzle and replace the lid after use so that your paint and glue don't dry out.

fashion and style

Are you are fashionista? *Do you have a very strong sense of style and love to accessorise? Well here is a mix of stylish projects that you will be proud to wear and proclaim, 'I made this!' You could accessorise with hand-sewn jewellery, like the Mushroom Brooch or the Jellyfish Pendant, or set your own trends with the Colour Block Belt or Patchy Scarf to match your favourite outfit. So grab a glass of fresh lemonade to give yourself some energy, scour the fabric box to get some inspiration and start creating!*

mushroom brooch

pencil pouch

jellyfish pendant

embroidered keyring

illustrated softy badges

colour block belt

patchy scarf

not just a bag

Mushroom Brooch

Mushrooms have a mysterious, magical appeal. They often show up in fairytales, nursery rhymes and adventure stories. Next time you go on an adventure, or are on a mushroom-hunting expedition, wear this fantastic brooch you have made yourself.

project by: tabitha patterson
suitable for: beginners
should take: 1 hour

SHOPPING LIST

- Cream or plain cotton/linen fabric for the back of the mushroom (20 × 12 cm)
- Spotty cotton fabric for the underside of the mushroom (8 × 5 cm)
- Coloured cotton or linen for the top of the mushroom (8 × 5 cm)
- Coloured cotton or linen for the spots (5 × 5 cm)
- Fusible interfacing (10 × 12 cm)
- Sewing thread (to match your coloured fabric)
- Contrasting thread for the outline stitching
- Metal brooch back (or a safety pin)
- Paper

CRAFTY NEEDS

- Sewing machine
- Fabric scissors
- Iron
- Needle
- Baking paper

TEMPLATES

You will need the Mushroom Brooch template for this project.

TECHNIQUES

Running stitch, page 9
Using fusible interfacing, page 14

NOTES

- Use small fabric scraps, be creative and make all sorts of different colour variations.
- If you can't obtain brooch backs, simply stitch a safety pin onto the back of your mushroom.
- Make sure you have your iron set up and ironing board out before starting.
- When ironing on interfacing, place a cloth, like a clean teatowel or pillowcase, between the interfacing and the iron, to protect the iron.
- This is a very easy project to make completely with hand-sewing, but it is equally fine to make some of it with a sewing machine.

HOW TO MAKE

1. Trace all of the pattern pieces onto paper, then trace the pattern onto your fabric and cut out the fabric pieces.

2. Layer your pieces on top of each other. The stem goes over the spotty fabric (see diagram 1), and the top mushroom piece goes on top of the stem and spotty piece (see diagram 2).

3. Cut out your piece of interfacing into a square. Lay the wrong side of the layers of pieces of fabric that make up your mushroom onto the rough side of the interfacing (see diagram 3). Turn it all over and iron the interfacing onto the back (this will hold the pieces together). Use baking paper to prevent the interfacing from sticking.

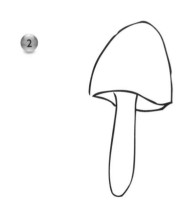

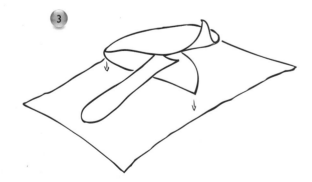

4. Trim the fusible interfacing away from the edge of the mushroom (see diagram 4). Cut out your spots and place them on the mushroom. Hand-stitch using a running stitch, making small stitches around the spots (see diagram 5).

5. Stitch the mushroom around the outside edges onto a piece of cream fabric (see diagram 6). You can do this by hand, using the same running stitch and small stitches as before, or use your sewing machine. Use a dark contrasting thread to outline the mushroom. Cut away the excess fabric and sew your brooch back onto the reverse side (see diagram 7).

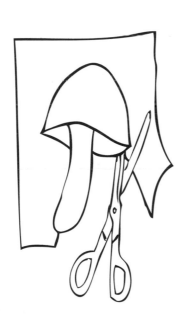

Pencil Pouch

This quick pouch is really functional – it would be great for the artist to carry coloured pencils, or for the music lover to carry their iPod. Crafty types can also make extras for their lip gloss, glasses or tissues. With no complicated closure this pouch is a super-easy project, and you could make one to fit whatever you carry.

project by: laura lynn wilson
suitable for: beginners
should take: 1 hour

SHOPPING LIST

- 2 pieces of cotton fabric – the size depends on what you are making, as follows:
- Pencil pouch (13 × 50 cm); iPod pouch (15 × 21 cm); Make-up pouch (26 × 15 cm)
- Ribbon for loop
- Sewing thread

CRAFTY NEEDS

- Sewing machine (or needle and thread)
- Fabric scissors
- Pins
- Iron

TECHNIQUES

Hand stitches, page 9

NOTES

- For a custom sized pouch, measure the item's width and height then double the width and add 3 cm to the height and width.
- Use any woven fabric you like! If you use a bulky fabric like corduroy, make your second fabric lighter weight so your seams aren't too bulky. Choose fun colours for both the outside and inside. The inside fabric will show on the edges and whenever you open the pouch!
- It helps to iron the fabric as you go.

HOW TO MAKE

1. Cut two rectangles for your pouch using the standard measurements above or customise the size for your own items.

2. Place the two pieces of fabric right sides together and pin together. Using your sewing machine set on a straight stitch (or use a small running stitch by hand, page 9) sew around the rectangle, leaving a 1 cm seam allowance, and remove the pins as you come to them. When sewing, begin in the middle of one long side, pivot your fabric as you come to the corners and leave a 10 cm gap open (see diagram 1).

3. Fold in the seam allowance on your corners and turn it right side out, through the 10 cm gap that you left. Poke the corners out neatly and iron your fabric, pressing in the seam line of the gap, and hand-sewing the gap closed using a whipstitch (page 9).

4. Decide where you want the opening of your pouch to be. For the iPod pouch, place the opening close to one edge to make it easier to slide the iPod in and out. For the pencil and make-up pouch, place the opening close to the top so that it opens like a crayon box. Fold the ends to where you wish to place the opening and overlap them about 1 cm (see diagram 2). Pin in place.

5. Cut a loop of ribbon 10 cm long. Fold it in half, and tuck the ends into one of the folded corners (see diagram 3).

6. Sew across the open edge, catching the ribbon and securing the overlapping pieces. Repeat on opposite edge (see diagram 4). All done!

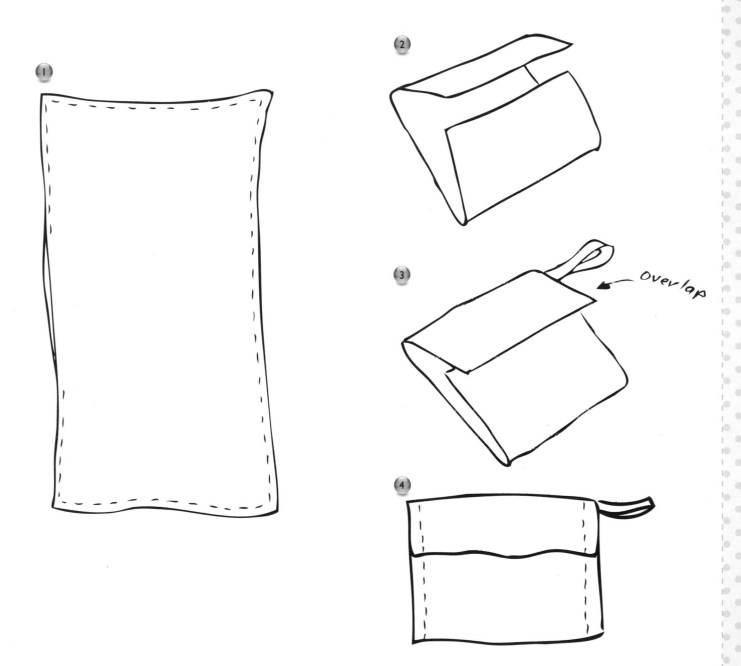

Overlap

Jellyfish Pendant

This little jellyfish won't sting! Made from plastic canvas with hanging thread 'tentacles', this sea creature will add a touch of whimsy to your wardrobe. You could also make a larger version as a hanging ornament. Once you become confident you can use the plastic canvas stitching techniques to make your own designs.

project by: ellen luckett baker
suitable for: beginners
should take: an afternoon

SHOPPING LIST

- White embroidery thread
- Plastic mesh canvas (10 count)
- Two small buttons, approximately 1 cm in diameter
- Pendant hook
- Silver chain or length of leather

CRAFTY NEEDS

- Small embroidery needle
- Scissors
- Small pair of pliers

TECHNIQUES

Cross stitch, page 10
Sewing a button, page 10

NOTES

- Plastic canvas can be purchased in different sizes (called 'counts') from a craft store.
- If you need to change your thread half way through, simply tie a knot on the back of the canvas and begin stitching again.

HOW TO MAKE

1. With your all-purpose scissors, cut the plastic canvas piece to be 2.5 x 4 cm and cut the corners of the plastic canvas as shown in the diagrams.

2. Thread your needle and tie off in a corner of the plastic canvas at the back. Start sewing from the back to the front; begin stitching a row of cross stitches, going in one direction only (see diagram 1).

3. Continue stitching rows until you have reached the top. Stitch over the tail of the thread to hide it on the underside.

4. Work back down toward the bottom and complete your cross stitches by this stitching in the opposite direction, forming an 'X' (see diagram 2). Continue until you have stitched all of the rows.

5. Working from the back to front, stitch along the edges. Continue until you have covered three sides of the plastic canvas (leave the bottom unstitched).

6. Create the tentacles. Fold a 15 cm length of thread in half and bring the loop end up through one of the squares at the bottom. Pass the cut ends through the loop and pull the loop tight (see diagram 3). Repeat until you have a tentacle in each of the bottom squares.

7. Sew two button 'eyes' onto the canvas by tying a knot in the back and pulling the thread through the buttonholes. Repeat for the other eye (see diagram 4).

8. Attach the pendant hook to the top centre of the canvas and pinch it closed with a small pair of pliers. String the pendant onto the chain.

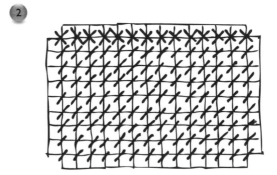

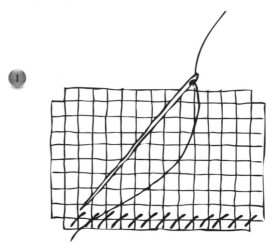

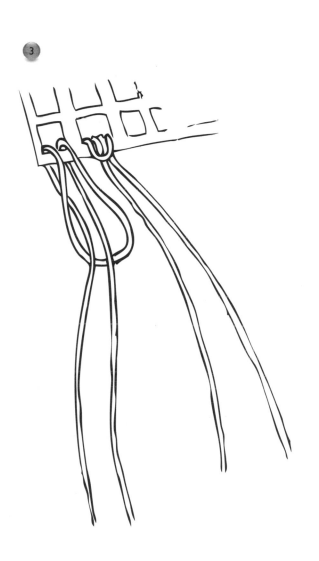

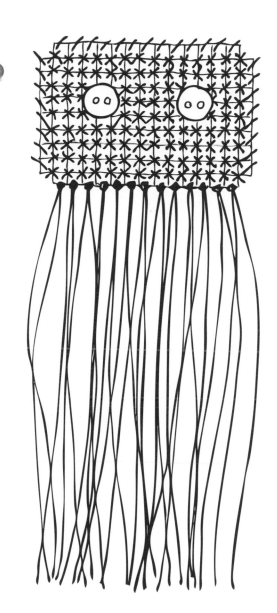

Embroidered Keyring

Using some faux wood vinyl off-cuts that you can find at the hardware store, you can make this tricked-out keyring. Or go even further and make a pendant, bag tag, necklace or bracelet. The designs embroidered on them can be anything you like. Try out emoticon designs — your friends will understand them but your parents won't!

project by: kirsty macafee
suitable for: confident beginners
should take: 2–3 hours

SHOPPING LIST

- Embroidery thread
- Off-cuts of flooring vinyl (ask at the hardware store)
- Sticky tape
- Paper
- Silver keyring loop

CRAFTY NEEDS

- Scissors
- Needle
- Nail
- Printer (optional)

TECHNIQUES

Hand stitches, page 9

NOTES

- Use a large and simple font for this if printing it from the computer.
- You won't need a hammer to pierce a hole, as the vinyl is soft and the nail just pushes through easily using your fingers.
- You can make a pendant or bag tag instead of a keyring. Simply attach some plaited thread or twisted cord to the vinyl in Step 4 instead of the keyring loop.
- Try these emoticons: :) :-) :D (-_-) <3

HOW TO MAKE

1. Cut out your keyring shape from the vinyl. Print or trace your emoticon onto paper. Tape your printout or drawing of the emoticon onto your keyring shape. Using a medium sized nail, pierce the design into the vinyl (see diagram 1). Make your holes at the intersection of straight lines or a couple of millimetres apart around curves. Remove the paper, but keep it alongside as a guide to join your dots when you begin stitching.

2. Thread your needle with embroidery thread and make a knot. Begin with the knot on the wrong side of your design. Use a backstitch (see page 9 for this stitch) to create your design into the vinyl (see diagram 2). Keep checking your paper guide to make sure you've got it right. To finish, knot the thread again on the wrong side of your design and thread the extra bits through the back of the stitches to prevent them from dangling and tangling.

3. Using your nail again, pierce holes around the outside of your stitched keyring about 1 cm apart. Blanket-stitch around the outside of the pendant to finish it neatly (see diagram 3).

4. Punch a small hole in the top of your keyring and attach the keyring loop.

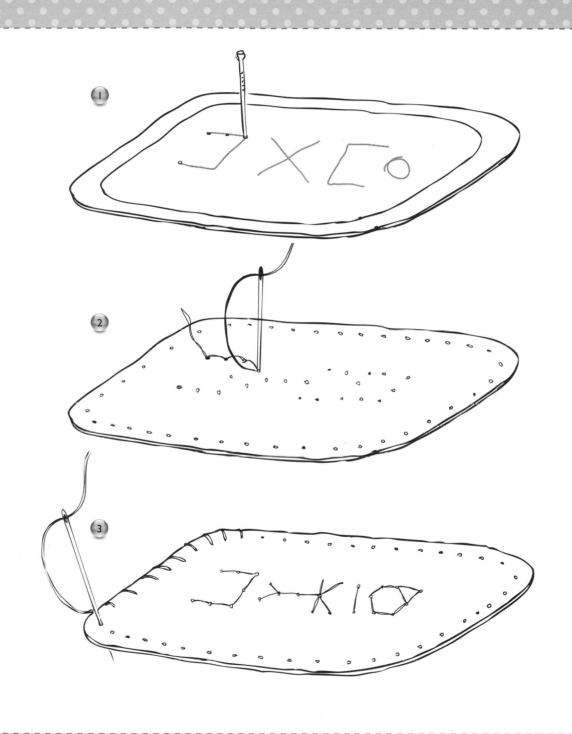

Illustrated Softy Badges

These awesome softy badges are created with your own art. Use your imagination and express yourself with drawings or words. Colour them in and add some hand stitching, wear them on your bag, your shirt or your hat – mix it up and have some fun!

project by: lisa tilse
suitable for: beginners
should take: 2–3 hours

SHOPPING LIST

- Cotton fabric scraps – plain or printed
- Sewing thread
- Brooch backs (from craft supply stores)
- Velcro
- Pillow stuffing
- Cotton balls (optional)
- Paper

CRAFTY NEEDS

- Fabric scissors
- Pins
- Sewing machine (optional)
- Needle
- Chopstick
- Iron
- Felt-tip markers

TECHNIQUES

Hand stitches, page 9

NOTES

- You don't need to be an artist to create great badges. Words, initials and abstract shapes work well too.
- Calico is inexpensive and good for drawing on. Alternatively, use scraps of old clothes or bed sheets. Cotton, poly-cotton and linen are best for this project.
- If you're making a few small badges you could use cotton balls (from the supermarket) to stuff them but they won't be washable. Tease the cotton balls apart before using them so they don't form hard lumps inside your badge.
- Instead of a brooch back, sew a ribbon loop on your illustrated softy to hang it from your school bag or bedroom door handle. Or sew a velcro loop on the back to attach your badges to a bag strap.

HOW TO MAKE

1. Spread out your fabric and place some paper or newspaper underneath in case the markers bleed through onto your work surface.

2. Start creating! Draw and write. Doodle. Have fun. The best size for your illustrations is between 4 cm and 9 cm. Make sure you leave about 5 cm between each illustration to allow space for cutting out and sewing.

3. Choose which of your illustrations you'd like to turn into badges. Draw a line around each one with pencil, leaving a clear space (about 2 cm) all the way around. Cut out along the lines.

4. If you'd like to add some hand-stitched details, now is the time.

5. Choose fabric for the back of your badges. You could even create your own patterned fabric with your felt-tip markers, or use some cool fabric you like. Place the front and the back pieces right sides together and pin them. Trim the backing fabric the same size as your front piece.

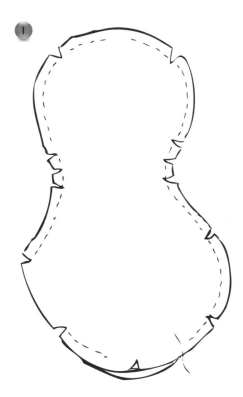

6. Sew the front and back together about 0.5 cm in from the edge, leaving a small gap of 2.5 to 3.5 cm open so you can turn the badge right side out. The gap is best placed on a straight edge if possible. Cut small notches into the seam allowance, being careful not to cut into the seam line (see diagram 1). Turn the badge the right way out. If you have any tricky corners, use a chopstick or the blunt end of a pencil to help push them out. Fold in the open edges and iron the badge flat.

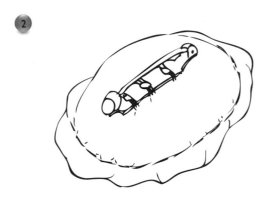

7. You could also hand-stitch the front and back together, wrong sides facing, leaving the raw edges of the seam showing on the outside. If you would like to try this method, use a small neat running stitch and a brightly coloured thread.

8. Using small pieces of pillow stuffing, stuff your badge. It shouldn't be too full or hard. Fold in the open edges of the gap and pin. Hand-stitch it closed using a whipstitch.

9. Firmly hand-sew the brooch back (see diagram 2), or your ribbon or velcro loop (see diagram 3), onto the back of the softy. Make some extra badges for your friends.

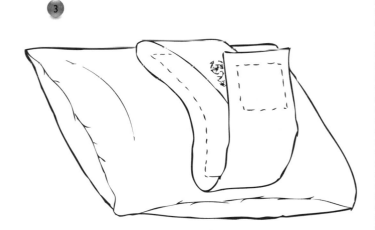

Colour Block Belt

Mix and match different colours, textures and patterns to make this cheerful belt from blocks of bright fabric scraps. All you need is a sewing machine, some fabric and belt hoops which you can recycle from second-hand belts and you will have yourself some super cool and unique gear to wear anywhere.

project by: kathreen ricketson
suitable for: beginners
should take: 2–3 hours

SHOPPING LIST

- Scraps of cotton fabric in various colours
- Strip of cotton fabric (7 × 100 cm or the length and width of your finished scrap belt strip)
- 2 × D-rings (from craft or hardware stores) for the belt buckle
- Sewing thread

CRAFTY NEEDS

- Sewing machine
- Chopstick
- Iron
- Pins

TECHNIQUES

Hand stitches, page 9

NOTES

- You could use any fabrics and colours you like here, but I think it is best to stick with washable cotton fabric and a palette of three or four colours that you like.
- The fabric for the belt back could also be made of more scraps or you can choose a single fabric to coordinate.
- Use a buckle that is a fold-through kind (such as the D-rings) intead of the sort that means you need to punch holes in your belt.
- To make a standard belt, 100 cm will be long enough, but if you need your belt to be longer or shorter, then measure the waist or hips of the person who will wear the belt and add an extra 40 cm.

HOW TO MAKE

1. Cut all your scraps of fabric 7 cm wide and as short as 4 cm or as long as 20 cm. Lay them all out on your bench, length to length until they measure approximately 100 cm.

2. Once you have laid out all your scraps and arranged them to your liking, sew the pieces together, one by one. Place each piece on top of the next, right sides together, and sew along the 7 cm side. Take your next piece and sew onto the next side, and keep going until all the pieces are sewn together in one long strip. Iron all the seams to one side so that your belt is flat.

3. Cut out a piece of fabric the same width and length as your sewn strip; this is for the back of the belt. Place your patchwork strip face up on your workbench and your backing strip right side down over your strip. Align the edges carefully and pin all around. Sew around the two long sides and one end, leaving one end open. This will create a long fabric tube.

4. To reduce bulk at the corners of the tube, clip the corners of the sewn short end. Use a chopstick to start turning the strip right side out (see diagram 1). Once your tube is longer than your chopstick, pull on a different part of the fabric until the tube is turned right side out completely. Use your chopstick to push out corners at the end of the tube. Reshape your rumpled tube and press along the length to form a neat belt.

5. Fold in the ends of the open end and press the seams. Sew up the open end and then top-sew around the edges of the entire belt.

6. Fold one end through both D-rings and fold down 10 cm towards the back. Pin in place then stitch through all layers (see diagram 2), stitching a cross pattern for extra strength (see diagram 3).

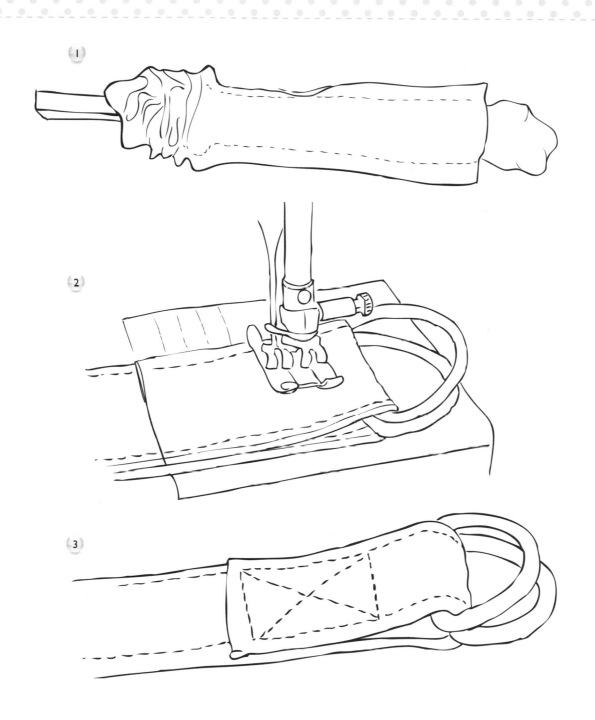

Patchy Scarf

This patchwork scarf is a great way to use up your favourite fabric scraps or bits of fabric cut from a much-loved piece of clothing that has worn out or no longer fits. You will have a stylish scarf that matches every outfit!

project by: heather elizabeth
    abernathy graham
suitable for: beginners
should take: 2–3 hours

SHOPPING LIST

- Fabric scraps
- Sewing thread

CRAFTY NEEDS

- Sewing machine
- Scissors
- Needle
- Pins
- Iron

TECHNIQUES

Hand stitches, page 9

NOTES

- Alternating patches of dark and light colours will make the patchwork really stand out. For a subtle look, choose fabrics that are similar in colour.
- Before you start to cut out the pieces, try arranging different combinations of fabric scraps to see what you like best. You may want to cut a few more squares and rectangles than you actually need, so you have more options while you are arranging the pieces.

HOW TO MAKE

1. Cut out 18 squares (14 × 14 cm) and 16 rectangles (14 × 8 cm) from the fabric scraps.

2. To arrange the patches, first line up the patch pieces for the front and the back of the scarf on the floor or a long bench. You will have one row for the front of the scarf and one row for the back; you should have 9 squares and 8 rectangles in each row. Start both rows with a square then alternate square, rectangle, square, rectangle, and so on. When you are happy with your arrangement, stack up the pieces (one stack for the front and one stack for the back, as in diagram 1). Be careful to keep the pieces in order.

3. To sew the patches together, start with the square at the top of the stack. Pin the next piece (a rectangle) to the first square with the right sides together. Using a straight stitch, machine-sew the first two pieces together along the side, removing the pins as you come to them (see diagram 2). Continue pinning and sewing the patches together in this way, adding one piece at a time (see diagrams 3 and 4). Do this for the front and back of the scarf, and then iron your sewn strips so the seams lay flat.

4. To sew the front and back of the scarf together, first lay the front of the scarf right side up on your bench, and lay the back of the scarf right side down on top of it. Line up the edges carefully and pin all around. Machine-sew the front and back together, sewing along one side, turning to sew one end and then sewing along the other side. Leave one end open (see diagram 5). When you finish sewing you should have what looks like an inside-out tube with one end closed and one end open.

5. Turn the tube right side out and press it flat, poking out the corners with a chopstick. At the open end of the tube, fold the raw edges inside about 1 cm. Carefully press the folded edges. Hand-stitch the folded edges closed using a whipstitch and matching thread so the stitches are not too obvious. Press the entire scarf and you are done.

Not Just a Bag

You can't have too many bags! With these instructions you can make one for every activity. Use heavy-weight canvas or denim to make it extra strong. The loops and straps allow you to use the bag as a backpack or a messenger bag. Add a ribbon closure or buttons with elastic loops and head off with your new bag to the library, the pool, soccer practice, or a sleep-over.

project by: pascale mestdagh
suitable for: confident beginners
should take: an afternoon

SHOPPING LIST

- Cotton fabric of your choice cut as follows:
- One rectangle (36 × 96 cm) for the body of the bag
- 3 strips of fabric (each 7 × 15 cm), or 3 cm-wide ribbon for loops
- 1 long strip of fabric (150 × 7 cm) for the shoulder strap, or 2.7 m of cotton rope)
- 4 interesting buttons and 2 elastic hair bands in a matching colour, for closure
- Matching sewing thread

CRAFTY NEEDS

- Sewing machine
- Fabric scissors
- Pins
- Ruler and measuring tape
- Large safety pin
- Needle

TECHNIQUES

Hand stitches, page 9
Sewing a button, page 10
Making a French seam, page 11
Making binding, page 18

NOTES

- The bag when finished measures 45 × 31 cm; with flap closed: 35 × 31 cm
- Keep this bag minimal by using plain fabric and decorating the finished bag with badges, fabric paint, glitter, ribbon, embroidery and so on. Or you could start out with colourful fabric. Make sure you use a strong fabric, like denim, heavy-weight cotton or canvas, heavy-weight linen, or corduroy.
- Either make the bag with four loops on the sides allowing for double use as a backpack or messenger bag, or omit either top or bottom loops depending on whether you prefer a backpack only or a messenger bag only.
- You can make your own loops with strips of fabric, or you can use wide, ready-made cotton ribbon. To make your own loops, choose a matching fabric then make the binding using the instructions on page 18. Sew the binding together down the length to create a neat strip of material.

HOW TO MAKE

1. To make the body of the bag, first take the large rectangle and sew hems along both of the short ends (see diagram 1).

2. Place this rectangle in front of you, with the right side of the fabric facing up. Place the loop or cotton ribbon about 12–14 cm from the top hem. Make sure the loop points down. Pin into position then sew into place. Next, fold the loop upward, pin and then sew into place once more (see diagram 2).

3. Fold the body of the bag in half, with the right side facing you and the fabric fold closest to you (see diagram 3). Fold the two other strips (or ribbon) in half. Pin them to the bag, on the same fabric side as the top loop, about 2–3 cm from the bottom fold near you and with their fold pointing to the centre of the rectangle (see diagram 4).

4. Sew closed the side seams using a French seam closure, as follows. With the right side of the fabric still facing you in the same way as in the previous step, pin both side seams closed on the right side of the fabric. Now, sew both side seams closed, using a narrow (1 cm) seam allowance. By doing this, the loops you pinned onto the fabric in Step 3 will be stitched into place as well.

5. Turn the bag inside out, and trim your seams a little. Pin the side seams, tucking the previously sewn seam neatly inside. This time sew the side seams using a wider (1.5 cm) seam allowance. Turn the bag inside out. The loops are tucked inside both seams, making them extra strong.

6. Fold the top 10–12 cm of the bag toward the front of the bag, making this the flap of the bag.

7. Make your button closure. Cut the elastic hair band open and pull it through the button's holes. Tie a little knot at both ends of the elastic so the button can't slip off. Mark the spot where you want

to place the button – the same side of the fabric as where the back loop is. Hand-sew the elastic hair band into place with a couple of stitches right below the knots. Push your button down by pulling the elastic loop and sew your button on top of the knots in the elastic to hide the knots and stitches. Next, fold over the flap again to determine where the buttons need to come at the front of the bag. Make sure this set of buttons is perfectly aligned opposite the first set of buttons (with loops) on the flap. Sew them into place.

8. Attach the strap to the bag or use the cotton rope. For a messenger bag fold your strap or rope in half and attach it with a knot to the top loop. For a backpack thread the strap or rope through one of the bottom side loops, up through the middle top loop and back down to the other bottom side loop. Work your way back, threading the rope in the opposite direction back to the first loop where you finish by knotting both ends together.

play and party

The projects in this section are fun and frivolous *and perfect for amusing yourself on a rainy day, or for getting together with friends and having a blast. The Bendable Bunny Ears will make a super addition to your dress-up box, but would be equally good to wear when you need cheering up. There are some plush friends to make in this section too — Limby the Button-eye Dude has lots of possibilities for variations, Happy Bat Buddy will keep you amused and Sassy the Sock Softy is great. Plus, you can make a checkers board — for playing checkers with your grandpa or as a gift for your checker playing companions. So get a cup of chocolate chai tea and some fresh buttercake, grab your fabric bag and sewing kit, and get cracking!*

bendable bunny ears

limby the button-eye dude

happy bat buddy

checkers board

sassy the sock softy

Bendable Bunny Ears

These bunny ears are fun and easy to make and are the perfect addition to your dress-up or party box. There's some extra cuteness because the ears are bendable, so you can have sad floppy ears, or perky curious ears – it is up to you and your inner bunny!

project by: georgia robinson
suitable for: confident beginners
should take: 1 hour

SHOPPING LIST

- Fun faux fur (25 cm square) in white (or any colour) for the outside of the ear
- Satin (25 cm square) in pink or your favourite colour for the inside of the ear
- Thin craft wire (two sections 65 cm long), obtain from a craft supply shop
- Plain plastic headband
- Strip of white slightly stretchy fabric or ribbon 3.5 cm wide and 1 m long, (similar to T-shirt material) to wrap around your headband.
- Sewing thread

CRAFTY NEEDS

- Needle
- Sewing machine (optional)
- Fabric glue
- Pliers
- Wire cutters
- Pins
- Fabric scissors

TEMPLATES

You will need the Bendable Bunny Ears template for this project.

TECHNIQUES

Hand stitches, page 9

NOTES

- These can be made in any colour combination (think grey and black, or blue and pink, or purple and silver).
- You can make smaller ears (think fox, puppy or kangaroo) by trimming the bottom of the pattern by 4 cm.
- This project can be made on the sewing machine, but is even easier if sewn by hand using a simple running stitch.

HOW TO MAKE

1. Use the large template to cut four of the triangles from the faux fur. Use the smaller template to cut two smaller triangles from the satin.

2. To form the front of the ears, place a small satin triangle over a faux fur triangle, with the wrong side of the satin sitting on the right side of the fur. Line up the bottom edge of the triangles, leaving a 3 cm border around the top edges, and pin them together (see diagram 1). Repeat with the other piece of satin and another faux fur triangle.

3. Sew around the edge of each satin triangle, removing the pins as you come to them.

4. Take the remaining faux fur triangle and place it, furry sides together, over the front of your satin-covered faux fur triangle (see diagram 2). Pin and then sew, either by hand or by machine as before, only around the top two sides of the triangle, and leave the bottom edge open. Repeat this process with the other two sections of fur.

5. Turn each of these ears right side out, creating two furry, triangular pockets. Trim the bottom edges to create a neat line.

6. Take your lengths of wire, and bend them in the centre. Place the wire inside each of the fur ear pockets, so that the wire lies snugly along the inside edge of each. Using your wire cutters, trim the ends of the wire to leave about 10 cm protruding from each side of the opening. Take five pins and pin the wire as closely as possible to the inside edge of each ear. (It can be difficult to find the pins among the fur, keep count of how many pins you put in, and make sure to remove them all.)

7. To hold your wire in place, sew another line of stitches on top of your original line around the edge of the pink satin (see diagram 3).

8. Make a pleat on the bottom edge of the ear and pin into position, then hand-sew a couple of whipstitches over the top of each other, through all the layers at the pleat (see diagram 4). Sew a line of stitches along the bottom edge of each ear, close to the edge, but don't sew over the wire.

9. Wrap the white stretchy fabric around the headband, starting from one end and working toward the other, and cover it entirely. Use fabric glue to secure the loose edges at either end.

10. To secure the ears to the headband, place the ears one by one against the headband, leaving a 3–7 cm gap between the ears. Wrap the cut ends of wire around the band two or three times to hold the ears in place. Using wire cutters, snip off the excess wire and ensure the ends of the wire are folded in closely against the outside edge of the band, to avoid snagging. These raw wires can then be covered by wrapping sections of the remaining white fabric around them, again securing the ends neatly with the glue and making sure all raw glued edges are on the bottom side of the headband.

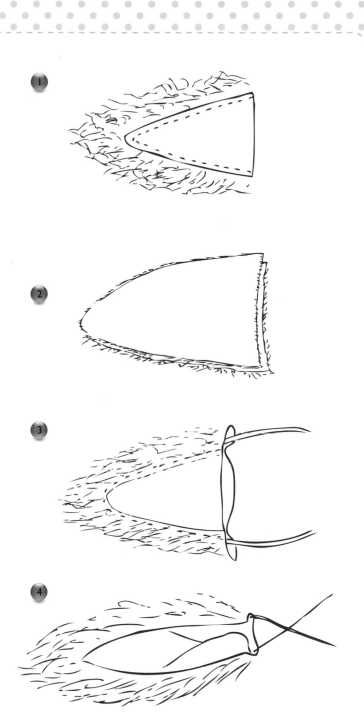

Limby the Button-eye Dude

Limby is a long-legged guy with button eyes. The original Limby was based on a drawing by an eight-year-old boy. Limby can be hand-sewn or sewn by machine, and can be customised to create a superhero character, spy, daredevil or anyone else you can dream up.

project by: lizette greco + grecolaborativo
suitable for: beginners
should take: 2–3 hours

SHOPPING LIST

- Scraps of cotton, wool or linen fabric in different colours
- Pillow stuffing
- Thread to match
- Buttons for eyes
- Paper

CRAFTY NEEDS

- Needle
- Sewing machine
- Pins
- Scissors
- Chopstick
- Pencil

TECHNIQUES

Hand stitches, page 9

NOTES

- Use a chopstick to turn the legs right side out and push the stuffing down into the legs.
- Limby can be entirely hand-sewn, but will be sturdier if machine sewn. Use a straight stitch on your sewing machine. You will need to hand-sew a whipstitch to attach the head and the legs to the body.
- Alterations can turn Limby into an action hero (like Super Daredevil) or a furry bedtime pal (like Cuddly Racoon). Make it green with one hanging button eye like a zombie (Zimby The Limby) or grey and silver like a robot (Robo-Cyclops). Create a whole new character by adding a moustache and some weights (like Pierre, the World's Strongest Man), a hat (like Nosy the Clown), or hair (like Tutu Girl).

HOW TO MAKE

1. Draw and cut out your Limby pattern pieces on paper. You will need: one body piece, 11.5 x 13 cm; two leg pieces, each 6 x 11.5 cm; and two head pieces, each 6 x 6 cm with rounded corners at one end. Pin your pattern pieces onto your fabric. Cut out the fabric pieces and set them aside.

2. Take the body piece and fold it in half. Sew along the edge (see diagram 1). Take each leg, fold in half and sew along the edges separately, closing one end at the feet (see diagram 2). Take the two head pieces and pin together with the wrong sides of the fabric facing each other. Sew around the head (see diagram 3).

3. Turn all the pieces right side out, use the chopstick to poke the fabric out fully and stuff them with pillow stuffing. You might need the chopstick again to push the stuffing into the legs and corners.

4. Pin one end of the body closed so the stuffing doesn't fall out. Take one stuffed leg and pin in place. Use a whipstitch to hand-sew around the leg, fixing it to the body (see diagram 4). Do the same with the other leg.

5. Pin the stuffed head to the body and hand-sew around the neck, fixing it to the body. Limby is now ready! You can sew on some button eyes, moustache, cape, yarn hair and so on (see diagram 5 for ideas).

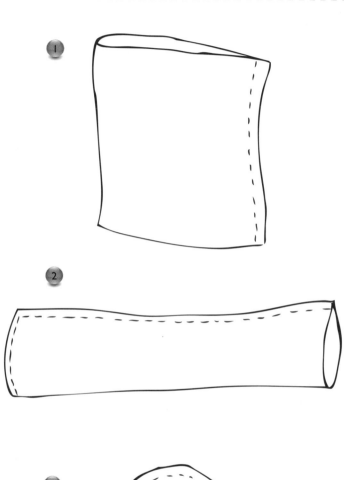

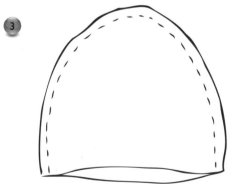

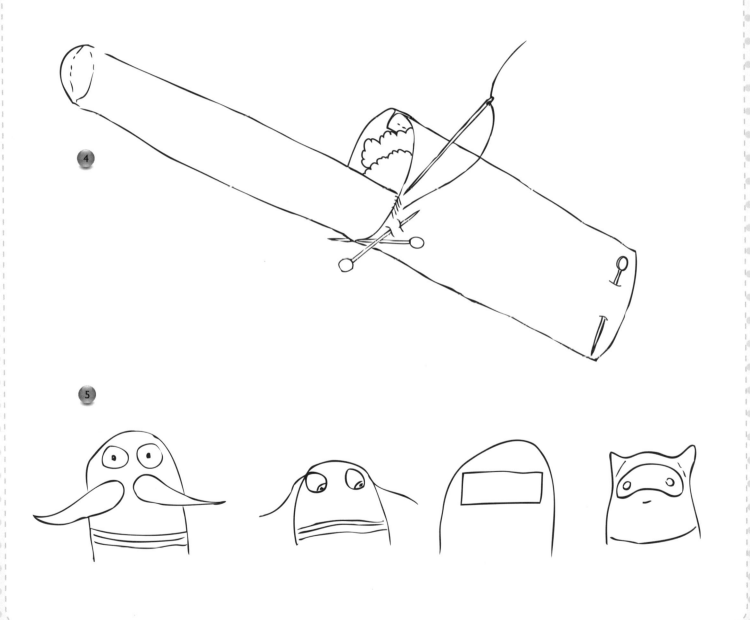

Happy Bat Buddy

Make your own happy bat buddy who is squeezable, huggable, tossable and lovable. Your bat buddy will happily guard your room, relax with you on your bed or accompany you on adventures. He loves to climb trees and flies through the air at a great speed!

project by: hannah rebecca fletcher
suitable for: beginners
should take: 2–3 hours

SHOPPING LIST

- Sturdy cotton fabric with a cool pattern or a pretty print for the body (30 cm square)
- Black felt, either wool or acrylic, for the wings (20 cm square)
- Pale coloured felt for the face to stand out against the body fabric. The felt will not fray or tear and the light colour will help the eyes and smile designs stand out.
- Pillow stuffing
- Sewing thread to match your bat's face and body
- Embroidery or sewing thread to contrast with your bat's face and wings

CRAFTY NEEDS

- Scissors
- Needle
- Chopstick
- Sewing machine (optional)
- Pencil and paper

TEMPLATES

You will need the Happy Bat Buddy template for this project.

TECHNIQUES

Hand stitches, page 9

NOTES

- This bat is very easy to customise. You can change the bat's facial features to give it a unique expression. You can mix up the colours and fabric to suit your personality. You can add other details to the bat's body such as felt cut-outs of your initials, or hearts and stars.
- This bat is equally easy to make with a sewing machine or by hand with a needle and thread.
- Use sewing thread to match your bat's colour. Use a contrasting thread to sew the wings and a different contrasting thread to sew the eyes and mouth.

HOW TO MAKE

1. Trace the pattern onto paper and cut it out. Lay the pattern pieces onto your fabric and felt, and trace around them with your pencil, then cut out your shapes. You will need to cut out two pieces for the body from the fabric, four wing shapes from felt, two ears and one face from felt.

2. Start by giving your bat a face. Using your pencil, lightly mark eyes and a smile onto the piece of felt that will become the bat's face. When you are happy with the face, thread your needle with a coloured embroidery thread that contrasts with your face colour, and sew over your markings. Use backstitch or running stitch. This is the fiddliest part of the entire bat, so take your time to make the eyes nice and large.

3. When you've finished the face, change your thread to a colour that matches the felt you're using for the face. Position the face onto one of the body pieces. Sew the face onto the body (see diagram 1). If sewing by hand you can use a whipstitch or running stitch; or if sewing by machine you can use a straight stitch or a zigzag stitch.

4. You're ready to begin the wings. Take two of the wing shapes you have cut out and pin them together so that they become one super-thick wing shape. Using a colourful contrasting thread, hand-sew the wings together around the edges. Do the same with the other two wing pieces. Layering the wings together in this way means they are much stiffer, and can stand out on their own (see diagram 2).

5. Lay the body piece (with the face sewn on) facing up on your bench. Lay the wings over the top, pointing inward and sticking out a little at the edge. Lay the ears pointing downward towards the bat's face. Hold the wings and ears in place with a couple of hand stitches (see diagram 3), then lay the other piece of the body over the top so the right side of the fabric is facing down. Pin the body pieces together. The ears and wings should be sandwiched in between.

6. Sew all around the bat, leaving a 10 cm gap at the bottom (see diagram 4), then turn him right side out.

7. Fill your bat with stuffing by using a chopstick to poke small pieces of stuffing inside the bat until he is full. Sew up the gap by hand, using a whipstitch.

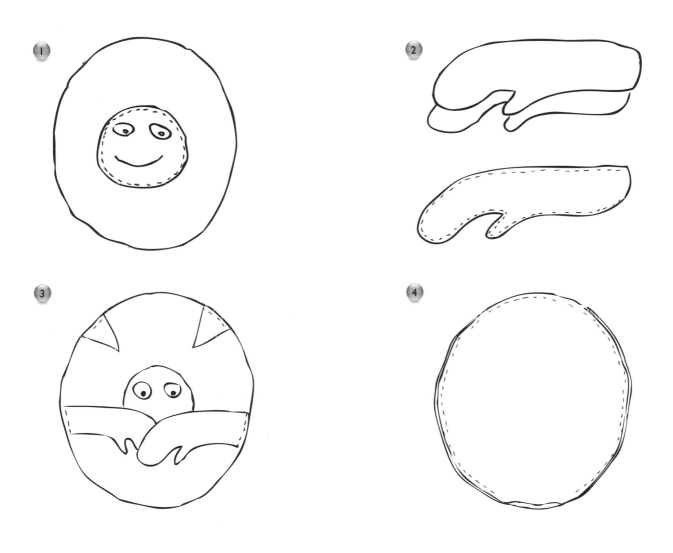

Checkers Board

Do you love to play checkers with your grandpa or best friend? Here is the perfect gift for yourself or your fellow checkers fans. Simply choose some of your favourite fabric and get sewing

project by: kathreen ricketson
suitable for: confident beginners
should take: an afternoon

SHOPPING LIST

- Light-coloured pattern cotton fabric
- Contrasting solid-coloured cotton fabric
- Batting (40 cm square)
- Backing fabric (40 cm square)
- Sewing thread

CRAFTY NEEDS

- Ruler
- Pencil
- Tailor's chalk
- Scissors
- Sewing machine
- Iron
- Needle
- Chopstick

TECHNIQUES

Hand stitches, page 9

NOTES

- This project is best made with two fabrics that are tonally different but that look good together, for example one fabric with a pattern and one that is a plain block of colour, in bold colours.
- Use vintage buttons as your checkers.

HOW TO MAKE

1. Use your tailor's chalk and ruler to measure and mark the wrong side of your fabric for cutting the strips. You will need your strips to be 7 cm wide and 50 cm long. Cut four strips of each of your two contrasting fabrics.

2. Sew your eight strips together, with the right sides of the fabric facing each other, along their lengths, alternating between the two different fabrics (see diagram 1). Using your iron to press the seams flat, go in one direction, so that your sewn block lies flat.

3. Take your ruler and pencil and mark 7-cm wide strips across the stripes. Cut these out; you should have eight strips (see diagram 2). Line up your strips on your bench to create a checkers board pattern (turn half of the strips around so the colours alternate). Take the first and second strip and pin them together at each seam, with their right sides facing.

4. Sew these first two strips together (see diagram 3). Repeat this process with the remaining strips, ensuring you sew them in the correct orientation so that the checkerboard pattern remains intact. Once this is sewn, press the seams so that the whole piece lies flat.

5. Measure your checkers board. It should be about 40 cm square (see diagram 4). Cut out your backing and batting fabric so that they are the same size as your quilt top. Layer the three pieces as follows: (1) quilt top facing upward; (2) quilt back, laying it face down onto the quilt top; and (3) the batting laid on top. Pin these three layers together all around the edge.

6. Use your sewing machine to sew around the outside perimeter of your pinned layers, but leave a 10 cm gap in one side. Trim your seams a little so they are not so bulky. Insert your hand into the gap, between the quilt top and quilt back, and pull the checkers board right side out. To make the corners square poke them out with a chopstick. Press the quilt top flat, and sew up the gap using a whipstitch.

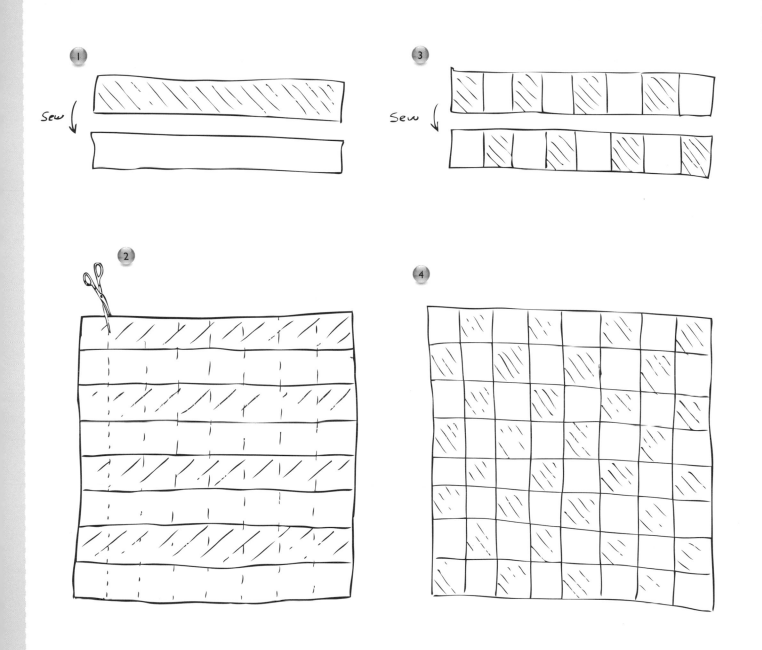

Sassy the Sock Softy

Grab a lonely and unloved stripy sock, and turn it into a sassy friend who can talk back to you. Sassy the Sock Softy is soft and cuddly but has an attitude and can out-chat anybody.

project by: holly keller
suitable for: confident beginners
should take: 2–3 hours

SHOPPING LIST

- 1 lonely knee-high sock
- Pillow stuffing
- Embroidery thread, black or white (contrasting to sock colour)
- Sewing thread to match the sock, plus pink sewing thread for the tongue
- 2 matching buttons
- 1 square of pink felt (12 cm square)
- 1 strip of felted fabric

CRAFTY NEEDS

- Scissors
- Sewing machine
- Needle
- Pins
- Pencil
- Chopstick

TECHNIQUES

Hand stitches, page 9

NOTES

- Because you really only need one sock for this project, you could use a pair and make two sassy friends.
- If you don't have a stripy sock, try using a sock with a contrasting toe and heel colour or a polka-dotted sock!
- This project also works well for hand-sewing. If sewing by hand, use small running stitches.

HOW TO MAKE

1. Cut up your sock pieces, using the diagram as a guide. Cut a notch in the sock piece that contains the sock heel – this part will become the body and legs of the softy. Cut the ear and arm pieces from the top portion of the sock.

2. Cut out a small piece of pink felt for the tongue (4 x 2 cm) and round off the corners of one end.

3. Take your four ear pieces and place in pairs, right sides together, and sew around the top and sides, leaving the bottom opening unstitched. Turn the ear pieces right side out then stuff them with your pillow stuffing. Repeat with arm pieces.

4. Take your stuffed ear pieces and hand-sew a running stitch around the top edge, then pull the thread ends to gather the top closed and make a couple more stitches to secure it in place.

5. Stitch together your two pieces of pink tongue felt that you cut out earlier. Sew a line down the centre of the tongue too. You can stitch this on your sewing machine, but because it is so small it might be easier to hand-stitch it using a running stitch. Firmly stuff the head piece (the toe of the sock), then hand-sew long running stitches along the top edge, pull the thread ends to cinch the top closed (as you did with the ear pieces), and secure with several stitches across the top.

6. Embroider the face design, using backstitch and your contrasting embroidery thread. Sew on the buttons as eyes. Use a whipstitch to hand-sew the tongue and the ears in place.

7. Sew the leg opening on the body closed by hand using a running stitch or whipstitch. Stuff the body, sculpting a little pot belly by placing more stuffing in the belly area. Be sure to get the stuffing all the way into the legs, using a chopstick to poke it down. Sew around the top edge, using long running stitches, then pull the thread ends to cinch the top of the body and secure it closed with several stitches across the top.

8. Use a whipstitch to attach the head to the body and the arms to the body on either side. Use your embroidery thread to sew a small 'x' on the belly to mark a belly button.

9. Make a scarf from a strip of felted fabric, then tie it around the neck to finish off your Sassy.

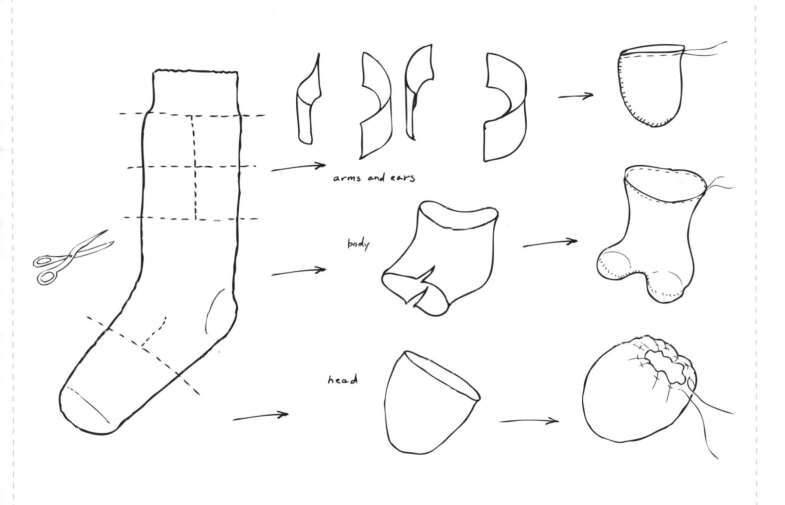

arms and ears

body

head

read and relax

Do you love to curl up in bed on a rainy day with a good book, or spend time writing in your diary and sending letters to friends? Or are you more into listening to music on your iPod? Here is a bunch of projects that will satisfy your craving for a quiet and relaxing space. Make some cosy pillows and cushions to lounge around on while listening to music with friends, or make an iPod Creature Cosy to house and protect your iPod. Make a Notebook Cover to personalise your diary or conjure up a fun Monster Reading Pillow with extra long arms to wrap around you! But before you can settle down to your read-and-relax session, get creative first. Make yourself a hot marshmallow chocolate drink, and go get inspired by foraging in the fabric scrap bin.

cloudy day pillow

iPod creature cosy

pet pillow

notebook cover

pocket cushion

'x' marks the spot bookmark

shhh! it's a secret letter

monster reading pillow

Cloudy Day Pillow

You can make these clouds as big or as little as you like, using all kinds of fabrics including cotton, wool or corduroy. You could even use an old pair of pyjamas, felted sweaters or blankets for a soft fluffy feel. Once you have the basics of making cloud pillows, you can make just about any shape you like – circles, hearts, trees, logs or even lily pads.

project by: claire dollan
suitable for: beginners
should take: 1 hour

SHOPPING LIST

- Fabric – a non-stretch cotton or wool fabric enough to comfortably fit the template (about 50 cm square)
- Sewing thread to match
- Stuffing for your pillows

CRAFTY NEEDS

- Sewing machine (optional)
- Scissors
- Pins
- Pencil
- Needle
- Tailor's chalk or disappearing pen

TEMPLATES

You will need the Cloudy Day Pillow template for this project.

TECHNIQUES

Hand stitches, page 9

NOTES

- You can use different fabrics for the front and the back of your cloud shape.
- Use one of the cloud shapes provided here, or feel free to draw your own freehand design.

HOW TO MAKE

1. Cut out your fabric square to comfortably fit your template piece, and lay the fabric pieces right sides together.

2. Choose a cloud template and trace around the edge using tailor's chalk or disappearing pen (see diagram 1), making sure to clearly mark the 10 cm gap for the stuffing.

3. Pin the fabric pieces, right sides together, adding a pin every 5 cm to prevent the fabric slipping as you sew (see diagram 2).

4. Sew along the drawn line, removing the pins as you come to them, being careful to leave a 10 cm gap as marked along the bottom (see diagram 3).

5. Cut around the sewn shape, leaving a 1 cm seam allowance outside the lines. Carefully snip around the curves (see diagram 4), being especially careful not to snip too close – but don't panic if you do, just put it back under the sewing machine and make another little stitch line to re-enforce it.

6. Turn the pillow the right way out, by putting your hand into the 10 cm gap you left and pulling out the fabric. Flatten and ease the curved seams into shape, by wiggling the seam between your fingers, then press flat.

7. Stuff the cloud to your liking (full and hard or loose and soft). Use a chopstick to push the stuffing into all the curves. When finished, pinch the opening together and pin it closed; then use a whipstitch to hand-stitch the gap closed.

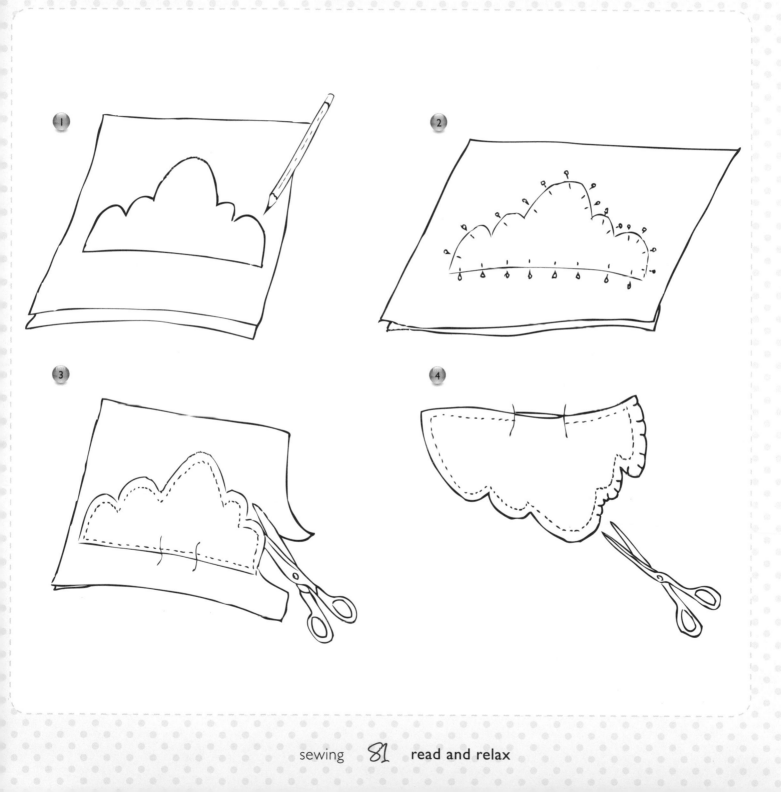

iPod Creature Cosy

If you have a soft spot for monsters – especially sweet and not so nasty monsters – this iPod case is for you. He is made from recycled sweaters and will keep your MP3 player safe and sound while you are not listening to it.

project by: holly keller
suitable for: beginners
should take: 1 hour

SHOPPING LIST

- White wool felt
- 12 cm square piece of felt from a felted wool sweater
- Black embroidery thread
- Sewing thread to match the sweater

CRAFTY NEEDS

- Scissors
- Needle
- Pins
- Pencil
- Chopstick
- Paper

TECHNIQUES

Hand stitches, page 9
Felting a wool sweater, page 11

TEMPLATES

You will need one of the iPod Creature Cosy templates for this project.

NOTES

- So long as you start with a 100% wool sweater it can be felted. Find wool sweaters at second-hand clothing shops, or ask your friends and relatives if they have any old ones to spare.
- You can customise the design of the monster's face however you see fit. There are three design templates included here, sized to fit either a standard iPod, an iPod Nano, or an iPhone.
- This project is small so it suits hand-sewing – just be sure to keep your stitches small and close together. Otherwise it can be sewn on a sewing machine.

HOW TO MAKE

1. Trace the monster template of your choosing onto paper and cut it out with paper scissors. Using a pencil, trace these paper template pieces onto your felted wool sweater. Cut out with your fabric scissors, taking care around the ears or horns.

2. Using a pencil, trace the eye and teeth templates onto your white wool felt and cut around these.

3. Pin the felt eye piece to the centre of the front head piece, where indicated on the template, and sew into place. Sew a couple of running stitches or a cross stitch into the centre of the eye using black embroidery thread. Repeat for the other eyes (see diagram 1 for ideas).

4. Fold the raw straight edge of the front head piece inside, by about 1 cm, and pin into place. Pin the felt teeth into place. Sew across the folded edge, by hand or with your sewing machine, taking care to capture the teeth into the stitches.

5. Place the back monster body piece so the right side of the sweater is facing up. Place the front monster head piece on top of this, so the wrong side of the head piece is facing up. Align your head edges on the two pieces and pin the front head piece in place to the back body piece. Place the front body piece on top of the front head piece and back body piece, again aligning the edges, so your two front body pieces overlap by about 2 cm, and pin in place (see diagram 2). When you look at your monster pieces, you should only see the wrong sides of the fabric (the right sides should be facing each other). Sew around the edge of the monster, sewing all pieces together. If hand-sewing, make additional reinforcing stitches around the edges where the two front pieces overlap to help secure them over time.

6. Unpin and turn the monster right side out through the overlapping edges. Using your chopstick, gently push out the horns/ears/any other facial features.

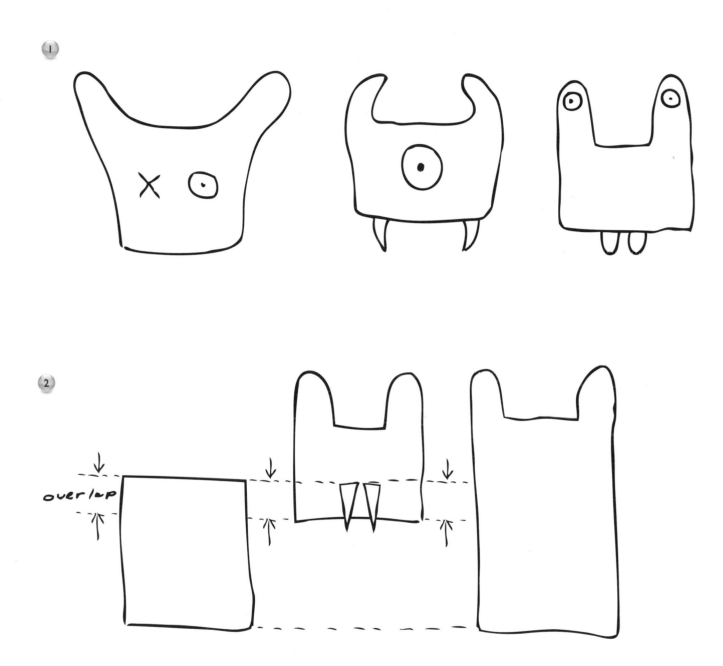

Pet Pillow

These cuddly pet animal pillows are perfect to take on a sleep-over or to just decorate your bed. Print your own pets' faces, a whole zoo or some creepy insects onto fabric and make your very own unique pillows. This project requires access to an inkjet printer (black and white is fine) and some sort of basic photo-editing software on a computer.

project by: karen jester
suitable for: beginners
should take: 2–3 hours

SHOPPING LIST

- 2 pieces of cotton fabric (each 45 × 55 cm) for the front and back of your pillow.
- Sewing thread to match
- Freezer paper or inkjet printable fabric
- Double-sided tape
- Regular printer paper
- Pillow stuffing
- Photograph suitable for image on pillow

CRAFTY NEEDS

- Inkjet printer (do not use a laser jet printer)
- For a washable pillow use permanent inkjet ink or use an inkjet setting solution
- Computer
- Iron
- Sewing machine
- Pins
- Scissors
- Ruler
- Needle

TECHNIQUES

Hand stitches, page 9

NOTES

- Customisation of this project is easy, you can choose different colour fabrics, and use fabric pens to draw glasses, bows or even a moustache on your pet.
- First of all you need to prepare your fabric to go through your printer. Regular fabric just won't work because it is too floppy and will get stuck in your printer. If you don't have any inkjet printable fabric, use freezer paper and follow the instructions provided – read up on where to get freezer paper and what you can use it for on page 14.
- When making the pillow, you will cut around your image to make different shaped pillows; however, if you have limited sewing experience consider making your pillow with straight edges. Sewing straight lines is much easier for a sewing beginner.

COMPUTER WORK

High contrast photos work best for this craft. Once you have selected your photo, open it in your photo editing software, and adjust its size to fit the paper size you will print on (such as A4 or letter). If you only have a black and white printer that's okay – make your photo black and white using your photo-editing software, and then adjust the contrast until you like your design.

Printer options

If your printer has a 'thick' or 'cardstock' paper option, choose it. And select 'best' print quality. Also select the 'fit to paper' option.

Before starting, check which way to place the paper in the printer. Test by drawing an 'x' onto a piece of regular paper and placing it right side up into your printer and printing your image. Now you know which way you should place your prepared fabric into the printer so that the image prints onto the fabric side.

HOW TO MAKE

1. Take a piece of printer paper and use this as your template. Cut your two pieces of fabric (for the front and back of your cushion) and a piece of freezer paper, just slightly bigger than your piece of printer paper.

2. Place your piece of front fabric right side down onto your ironing board and then place the piece of freezer paper evenly on top of it with the waxy side down. With a hot iron, no steam, iron the freezer paper until it is thoroughly attached with no creases. Pay close attention to the edges, making sure they are securely stuck down.

3. Take a piece of regular printer paper and neatly place double-sided tape all around the outer edges. Peel off the back of the tape and neatly secure to the back of the freezer paper. Cut away the excess fabric and freezer paper using the regular printer paper as your pattern guide. Place this piece of prepared fabric into your printer, correctly oriented so that it will print onto the fabric side. Print your

image on your fabric and let dry for 30 minutes on a flat surface. Remove paper and freezer paper backing. You will use this image to make your pillow.

4. Cut around your image, leaving a 1.5 cm border all around (see diagram 1). Place your backing fabric piece, right side up, on a flat surface. Place your fabric design piece, right side down, on top of it then pin it in place. Place pins every 5 cm to keep things from shifting when you sew. Sew around the edge of your pillow leaving a 10 cm opening on the bottom edge.

5. Trim the excess fabric on the back to match the front, being especially careful not to trim too close to the seams. On the curvy edges of your pillow, cut notches in your seam allowance about 1 cm apart, but do not cut all the way to your seam (see diagram 2). Turn your pillow right side out and fill it with stuffing. Using a needle and thread, hand sew the gap in your pillow closed with a whipstitch.

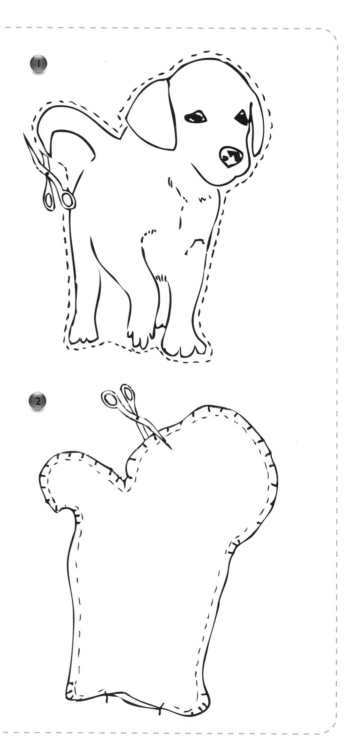

Notebook Cover

If you always use the same size notebook you can transfer your handmade book cover over to the new journal when you have filled it up. The pocket on the front is super handy for storing your pencils, and you can also slip paper notes into the inside flaps to keep them safe.

project by: kathreen ricketson
suitable for: confident beginners
should take: 2–3 hours

SHOPPING LIST

- A notebook – a small ring-bound book is perfect, such as an A6 notebook (12 × 15 cm)
- Enough fabric to cover the outside of your notebook and the same amount for the lining (43 × 16 cm)
- Sewing thread to match
- A small scrap of contrasting fabric for the outside pocket
- Thin elastic (about 20 cm)

CRAFTY NEEDS

- Sewing machine
- Scissors
- Pins
- Ruler

TECHNIQUES

Hand stitches, page 9

NOTES

- You will be using a sewing machine set on basic straight stitch for this project.

HOW TO MAKE

1. First measure your notebook while it is closed, all the way around from the front to the back. Measure the width of the cover then double it and add this measurement to the total and that is the length of your fabric. Measure the height of your notebook, add an extra 1 cm to all sides for your seam allowance and use this measurement to cut out your main fabric and your lining fabric.

2. To make your pocket, take your scrap of contrasting fabric and cut it the same height as your outer fabric and 7 cm wide. Cut a second piece the same size, then cut about 3 cm from the top of one of these pieces at a slight angle. Fold this edge over to the back and sew across the top. Place these two pieces on top of each other so the right sides of both pieces are facing upward and they are aligned at the base. Pin these together.

3. Take your main fabric and lay it out, right side up, on your table. Measure 15 cm from the left side and cut from top to bottom at this point. Pin your pocket piece with right sides together to each side of the cut you make then sew it in (see diagram 1). Press the seams. Place your backing piece right side down over this with the left sides aligned then trim the excess on the right-hand side (see diagram 2).

4. Take your elastic and cut to 16 cm long, or measure it to fit your book, cutting it to the height of your book and adding 1 cm. Lay out your main piece of fabric with the pocket sewn in and face it right side up. Lay your piece of elastic over your fabric in the same position as your pocket on the opposite side. Pin the elastic to the fabric. Lay down your backing fabric, right sides facing, and pin around the perimeter. Sew all around, being careful to sew the elastic in with the seams. Leave a 10 cm gap on one side.

5. Turn your piece right side out through the gap; the elastic should now be on the outside. Press your piece, being careful of the elastic. Sew the gap closed with a whipstitch. Press flat, and lay it out with the pocket side facing down, then lay your book open centred on the lining fabric. Fold the extra pieces over the book covers and pin into position. Do this for each side. Close the book and adjust the pinning so that the flaps close comfortably. Remove the book and sew the top and the bottom of the book cover – through all the layers (see diagram 3).

6. Place your book back in the cover and close it. Stretch the elastic over the book from the back to the front (see diagram 4). This will keep the book cover closed and you can also use the elastic as a bookmark if you like.

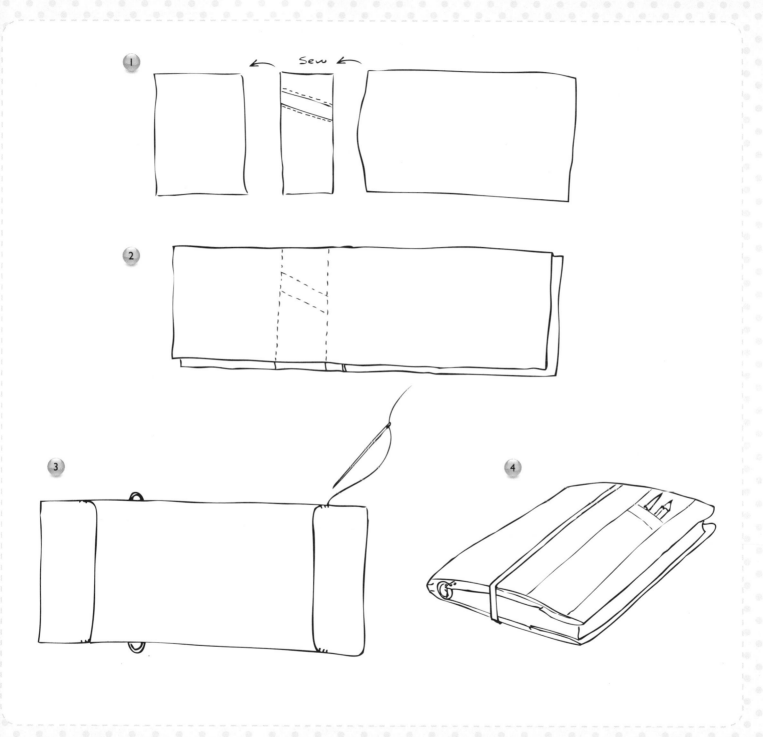

Pocket Cushion

This cushion is perfect for holding notes, money or secret treasures. Instead of old jeans, you could you could also use pockets from a funky shirt or even a coat. If you get really good at making these cushions, you can give them as presents – make one to hold the TV remote for your dad, or a block of chocolate for your best friend.

project by: sharon baldwin
suitable for: beginners
should take: 1 hour

SHOPPING LIST

- A pair of old pants, a coat, anything with a simple pocket on it and space around the pocket
- Matching or contrast fabric for the back of the cushion
- Sewing thread to match
- Stuffing for your cushion

CRAFTY NEEDS

- Sewing machine
- Needle
- Fabric scissors
- Pins
- Pencil
- Ruler
- Tailor's chalk

TECHNIQUES

Hand stitches, page 9

NOTES

- There are lots of different types of pockets – jeans pockets, coat and jacket pockets, pockets that close with buttons or velcro; have a look around the next time you go to a second-hand clothing shop or ask what old clothes you are allowed to cut up.
- Be sure to wash any clothes you find first, before cutting out.
- To make an entirely recycled cushion, look for old cushions or pillows at a second-hand shop and wash and dry before removing the stuffing to reuse for your own cushion.
- If you don't have access to a sewing machine you could hand-stitch these together.

HOW TO MAKE

1. Lay out your clothing with the pocket you want to use on a flat surface, like a table. With your tailor's chalk and ruler carefully draw a big rectangle around your pocket, as big as you can while still being on the fabric and not crossing any seam lines in the fabric (see diagram 1). You will need to have at least a 3 cm border around the pocket to allow room for cutting and sewing.

2. When you are satisfied that your chalk marks are straight and your cushion size will be big enough, use your scissors to cut carefully on your chalk line. Phew! That's the trickiest part done. You should now have a rectangular piece of fabric with a pocket on it.

3. Spread out the fabric for the back of the cushion, and lay your rectangle on top of it. Trace a chalk line around your rectangle onto this other piece of fabric and cut it out so that you have two squares of fabric the same size.

4. Place your backing fabric right side up and place your pocket rectangle right side down on top. Make sure all your edges line up, and place pins around the edges, every 2–3 cm, to hold them together (see diagram 2).

5. Use your sewing machine, set onto straight stitch, to sew around the edges, 1 cm from the edge. Leave a 10 cm gap so you can turn your cushion right side out (see diagram 3).

6. Turn your cushion inside out, using your fingers to poke out the corners and then fill with pillow stuffing. Hand-sew the gap closed, using a whipstitch.

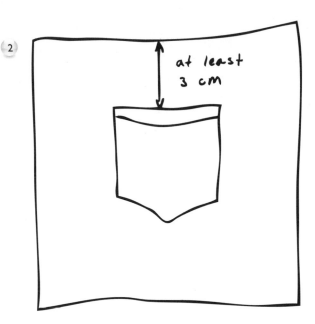

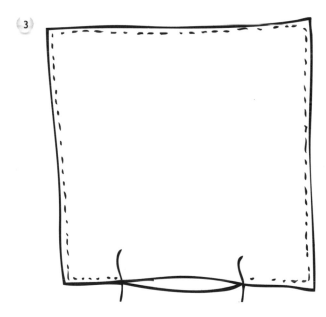

'X' Marks the Spot Bookmark

This bookmark looks really cool and will also protect your book. Make the 'X' with 'scribble stitch' — it's easy to do and looks like you've just gone over the 'X' with a pencil a few times. Once you get confident you can stitch any design you like — try a fancy 'X' using a font from the computer or use your own drawings and stitch the outlines with backstitch.

project by: kirsty macafee
suitable for: beginners
should take: 2–3 hours

SHOPPING LIST

- Cotton fabric
- Embroidery thread
- Scrap cardboard (such as a cereal box)
- Business card sized flexible magnet
- Glue
- Sewing thread

CRAFTY NEEDS

- Scissors
- Needle
- Iron
- Pins
- Pencil

TEMPLATES

You will need the 'X' Marks the Spot Bookmark template for this project.

TECHNIQUES

Hand stitches, page 9

HOW TO MAKE

1. Cut out your pressing template and card templates from cardboard. Cut your fabric 1 cm larger on all sides than your pressing template. Lightly trace an 'X' as indicated on the template, with pencil. Cut the flexible magnet and attach it to your card templates with glue (magnetic side facing out).

2. Using the pressing template, fold in the four fabric corners (see diagram 1). Next, fold in and press down the four edges of the fabric (see diagram 2).

3. Embroider your 'X' by making big straight stitches, just like cross stitch only bigger, going over and over again to get a scribbled effect. Be brave with your stitching, this is the creative bit.

4. Position your magnetised triangles of cardboard inside the pressed areas, leaving a 1 cm gap between the two magnets (see diagram 3). Fold the square in half along the dotted line to make a triangle. Then fold in half again to make a smaller triangle. Check that the magnets match up and that your 'X' is in the right place.

5. Open out the triangle and stitch the two open sides of the triangle together using a running stitch. This will keep the magnets in place. Fold the larger triangle in half again and blanket stitch the side of the bookmark closed (see diagram 4).

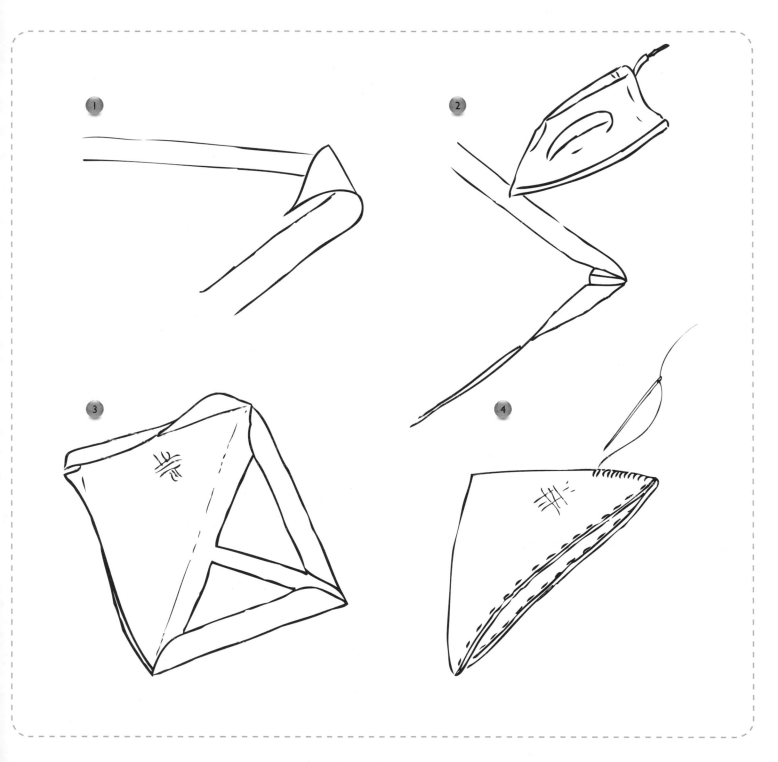

Shhh! It's a Secret Letter

This 'Secret Letter' can hold many special secrets – letters to friends, favourite trinkets or a special photo. It is so secret it should be hidden in the back of the drawer, swapped between friends or kept as a keepsake.

project by: shannon lamden
suitable for: confident beginners
should take: an afternoon

SHOPPING LIST

For the envelope:
- 2 pieces of contrasting cotton fabric (35 x 35 cm)
- 1 piece of plain cotton fabric (12 x 10 cm)
- Sewing thread to match
- 1 button (to match fabrics)
- 1 ribbon (10 cm long) for loop
- Fusible interfacing (optional)

For the letter:
- 1 piece of plain fabric (14 x 18 cm)
- 1 piece of contrasting fabric (14 x 18 cm)
- Embroidery thread

CRAFTY NEEDS

- Scissors
- Sewing machine
- Needle
- Pencil
- Pins
- Iron

TECHNIQUES

Hand stitches, page 9

i heard a secret,
and i promised
to only tell one.
and that is you!

NOTES

- Folded envelope size is 22 x 20 cm; Letter size is 21 x 15 cm.
- Use bright, contrasting printed fabrics mixed with plain fabrics.
- You can customise this pattern to make into any size – small letters, larger letters – depending on the amount of fabric you have on hand and what you want to use it for.
- This secret letter can also double as a purse or wallet, make-up bag or treasures keeper. It can be hung from the wall or door handle to hold keepsakes. It makes a great holder for presents of gift vouchers, or it can be a reusable envelope that is sent back and forth between family members.
- For a quicker project you can omit the embroidery letter portion and write a letter on paper or on fabric with a permanent marker instead.
- Using fusible interfacing for the envelope is an option that will make the envelope feel sturdier and sit more squarely. To use interfacing, iron the sticky side of the interfacing onto the wrong side of the fabric and proceed as per the pattern.

HOW TO MAKE

1. Pre-cut all your fabrics and lay them out before you. Decide which fabric you want on the inside of the envelope and which fabric for the outer. If you choose to embroider your letter and envelope front, complete all the embroidery first using a backstitch or running stitch.

2. If using interfacing, iron the interfacing onto the wrong side of one piece of fabric for your envelope.

3. Embroider, or write with permanent fabric marker, your message onto two plain pieces of fabric – one is for the front of the envelope and one for the secret letter that will go inside (see diagram 1).

4. Pin the letter to the backing fabric, with right sides facing. Sew around the outside leaving a 20 cm gap on one side. Turn it right side out and press. Hand-sew the gap closed using a whipstitch.

5. Pin the envelope fabric pieces with right sides facing each other. Place the ribbon loop in a corner of the fabric, facing inward inside the two layers of fabric (see diagram 2). Sew all around leaving a 20 cm gap on one side. Turn it right side out and press. Hand-sew the gap closed using a whipstitch.

6. Lay your square envelope fabric on its side with the loop facing upward, and fold each corner of the envelope inward, making sure the loop is now facing the bottom. Iron into an envelope shape. You should have a nice square envelope face on one side and folded-in triangles on the other (see diagram 3). Hand sew the edges together.

7. Pick a spot on the envelope face to attach your plain embroidered or written fabric. Pin and either machine or hand-sew. On the back side of envelope, hand-sew the button (see diagram 4).

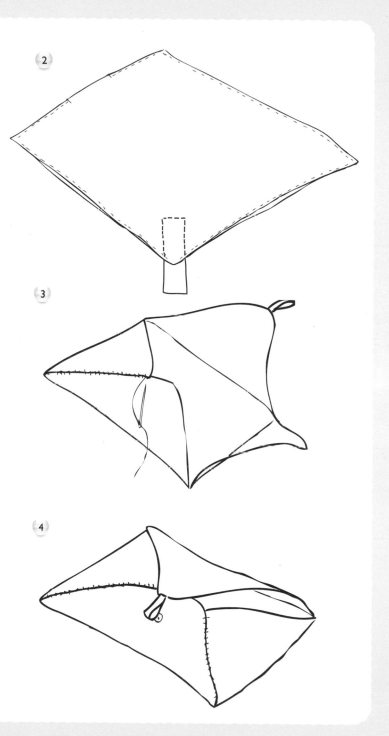

Monster Reading Pillow

Inspired by Max's friends from Where the Wild Things Are by Maurice Sendak, this pillow has long soft cuddly arms that can be wrapped around you while you read or sleep.

project by: khali whatley
suitable for: confident beginners
should take: an afternoon

SHOPPING LIST

- Striped or patterned cotton fabric for the body (60 cm)
- Plain flannel cotton fabric for the arms (80 cm)
- 5 coloured felt squares (12 cm each)
- Fabric glue
- Sewing thread to match
- Pillow stuffing

CRAFTY NEEDS

- Needle
- Sewing machine
- Fabric scissors
- Pencil

TEMPLATES

You will need the Monster Reading Pillow template for this project.

TECHNIQUES

Hand stitches, page 9

NOTES

- Feel free to design your own facial expression on your monster to make him totally unique.
- The project uses a straight stitch on your sewing machine, but could just as easily be hand-sewn if required.
- If you are very new to sewing, then you might like to make this guy without the arms. If you are quite confident of your sewing skills, you could sew on the felt facial features instead of gluing them to make your pillow completely machine washable.

HOW TO MAKE

1. Lay out your pieces of fabric with right side up. Fold the fabric in half so the right side of the fabric is on the inside of the fold. If you are using a striped fabric for the body of the pillow, check which way you want the stripes to go on your monster. Pin your pattern pieces to your fabric and use a pencil to trace around your pattern onto the fabric. Remove the pattern but keep your fabric pinned together. Use fabric scissors to cut along the outline of the pattern.

2. Sew each arm, leaving the ends open. Turn the arms right side out and stuff them to the elbow. Pin the arm at the elbow to keep the stuffing from moving and sew a seam along the width of the arm at this halfway point (see diagram 1). This will hold stuffing in place and create a bend in the arm. Finish stuffing your arm.

3. Cut out the face and the facial features (eyes, nose and teeth) of your monster from different coloured felt and use fabric glue to secure the eyes, nose and teeth onto the face (see diagrams 2 and 3). If you feel confident, sew these with your machine or by hand to make it super sturdy. Use more fabric glue to attach the monster face to the front of your monster body piece of fabric, or sew on the face to make it really secure.

4. Pin your arms to the front panel of the pillow and stitch in place. Pin the front and back pieces of the body together, with the right sides of the fabric on the inside. Leave a gap of 10 cm at the bottom of the pillow – you can let the long arms hang through this gap while you sew (see diagram 4). Sew all around the monster body, turning your sewing machine carefully when you come to the tips of the ears, but don't sew that 10 cm gap closed.

5. Turn your monster pillow right side out, through the 10 cm gap you left. It might help to pull the arms out first, then use a chopstick to poke the ears out, then stuff your monster dude with pillow stuffing. When the monster is full enough for your liking, hand-sew the gap closed using a whipstitch.

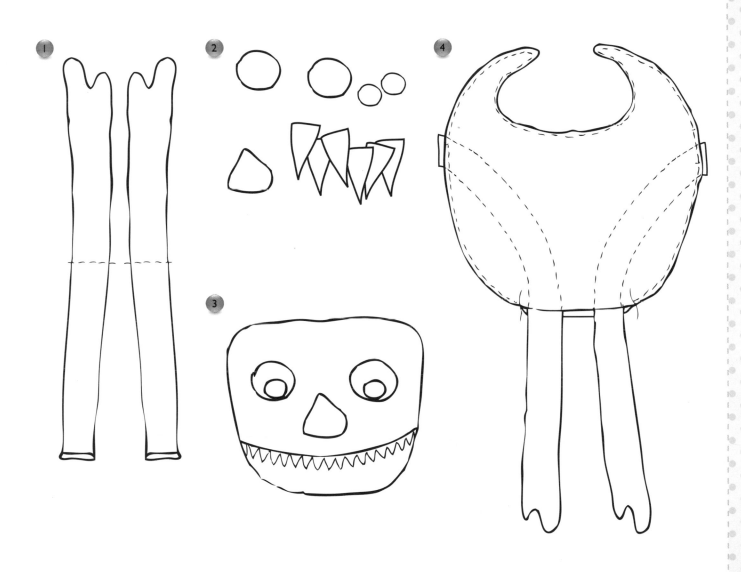

spruce your space

Is your room your castle? Do you have it decorated just as you like it, with posters, artwork and collectables stuck up all over the walls? These few projects will help you create some handmade happiness for your room. Make some Bunting Flags in all sorts of different colours to hang up around your room or even for your next party. Or, make some Linen Lavendar Birds and hang them from your window to make your space smell delicious. So if you want to get creative and spruce up your space, make yourself a nice cup of tea, grab some homemade chocolate brownies and become inspired!

linen lavender birds

bunting flags

sweet embroidered bird

hanging art pouch

Linen Lavender Birds

These fabric birds are filled with sweet lavender, so they will make your room smell lovely. If you want to make just one of these birdies you could add a brooch back and wear it. If you make a couple they'll be great to hang in your closet or wardrobe. Or, go all out and make this multiple-bird mobile/window hanging, which will add a cute touch to your room.

project by: joanna stott
suitable for: beginners
should take: 1 hour

SHOPPING LIST

- For each bird you will need one cotton or linen fabric rectangle (28 × 12 cm) for the body and one contrasting fabric square (12 × 12 cm) for the wing
- Sewing thread to match
- Pillow stuffing
- Lavender seeds
- Stick or dowel about 35 cm long from which to hang your birds
- Embroidery thread
- Paper

CRAFTY NEEDS

- Fabric scissors
- Pins
- Sewing machine
- Needle
- Pencil
- Tailor's chalk
- Funnel (optional)

TEMPLATES

You will need the Linen Lavender Birds template for this project.

TECHNIQUES

Hand stitches, page 9

HOW TO MAKE

1. Trace and cut out the templates onto paper. Fold fabric pieces for the body and wing in half with right sides facing in. Place your paper template on top then pin into place. Use your pencil or tailor's chalk to trace around your templates. Trace the wing onto the contrasting fabric twice. You will need to cut four wings and two bird pieces for each bird. Remove the paper template and replace pins inside the bird body. Cut out on your marked line. Repeat this process for your four wing pieces.

2. Leave pins in place and sew around the bird, leaving a 5 cm gap for turning the bird right side out. Repeat this process for both wings, remembering to leave a gap for turning (see diagram 1).

3. Clip notches into the seam around the bird and wings every 2 cm, being careful not to cut through the seam. This will help to keep the bird's shape once it has been turned.

4. Turn the bird body and wings right side out. Poke the beak and tail out gently using a chopstick. Fill each piece with stuffing. When stuffing the bird body, poke the stuffing first into the beak and tail, and then fill the rest with the lavender seeds (using a funnel will be helpful here). Finish the body with a little bit of stuffing at the opening of the belly. Use a whipstitch to close the gap.

5. Sew the wings to the body using a cross stitch at the top of the wing (see diagram 2).

6. Once you have made as many birds as you like, assemble your mobile – six is a good number to begin with. Cut your embroidery thread about 20 cm long and thread it onto an embroidery needle. Stitch one or two small stitches to the top of each bird (see diagram 3), and tie the top onto your piece of wood. Or you could cut the thread twice this length and sew the beginning and end of the thread to a bird each so they are attached to each end of the string, and then adjust the height and position of the birds until they balance. Tie a piece of string onto each end of your stick and hang it over your bed, in your closet or above your window.

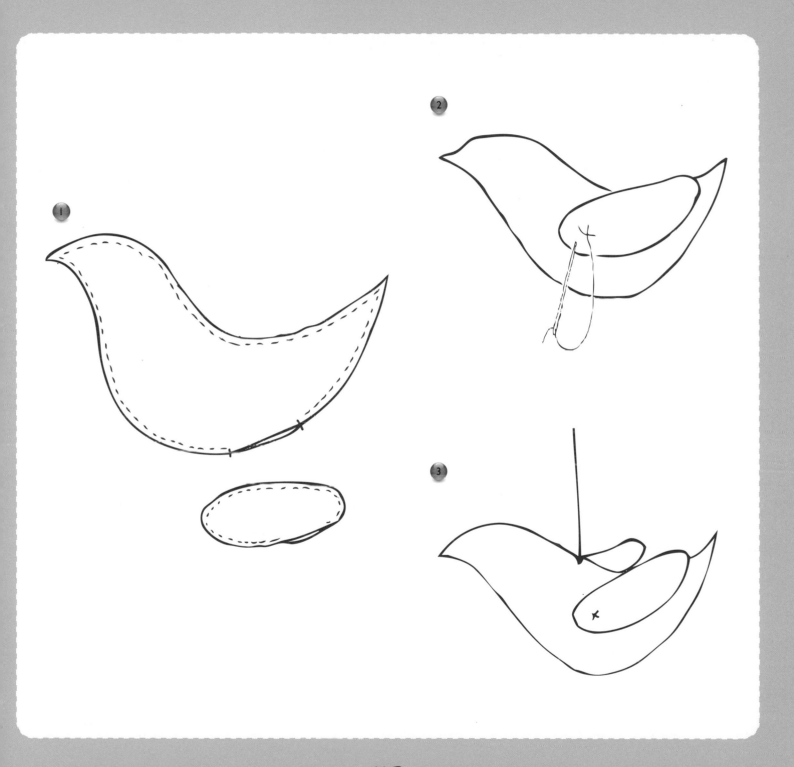

Bunting Flags

Bunting is a string of colourful flags. The flags can be made into any shape you like; triangles or squares are traditional, but you can make rounded and leaf-shaped flags in any fabric of your choice. Bunting is a sensational way to brighten your bedroom, or decorate the living room for a party.

project by: claire dollan
suitable for: beginners
should take: 2–3 hours

SHOPPING LIST

- Scraps of fabric (about 17 x 11 cm each)
- Sewing thread to match
- Binding (5 cm wide) in a colour to match your fabrics

CRAFTY NEEDS

- Sewing machine
- Scissors
- Pins
- Pencil
- Iron

TEMPLATES

You will need the Bunting Flags template for this project.

TECHNIQUES

Making binding, page 18

NOTES

- This project uses up scrappy pieces and left-over bits of fabric. If you don't have a fabric scrap bin to plunder, try using old clothing or even pillowcases and teatowels.
- Use pre-made binding that you can buy from your craft or sewing shop, or try the technique on page 18 that offers an easy way to make your own binding.

HOW TO MAKE

1. Lay your fabric pieces right side together, and place your scallop or leaf template on top of the fabric, with the top edge flush with the top edge of the fabric, and trace around it with a pencil. Cut these out; it will give you pieces that are exactly opposite each other.

2. Pin fabric pieces together then pin and sew around the curved edges, leaving the straight side unsewn (see diagram 1).

3. Carefully notch the curves (see diagram 2) and turn right way out. Flatten and ease the curved seams by wiggling the seam between your fingers and then ironing flat.

4. Repeat this process for as many scallops/leaves as you want to make.

5. Measure out the length of binding tape you need (this will vary depending on how many scallops/ leaves you would like to hang). Fold the tape in half lengthwise and iron (follow the same process if making your own binding tape).

6. Measure 30 cm along from one end of the binding tape and make a mark. This will be where you place the edge of your first flag. Tuck the bunting flag in between the binding, making sure the edges are flush, then pin in place (see diagram 3).

7. Pin the flags made earlier along the binding, leaving a 4–5 cm gap in between each flag. When you have added as many flags as you like, measure another 30 cm past the last one and cut the binding tape off. Pin the tape at the end.

8. When everything is pinned into place, use a zigzag or straight stitch to sew along the entire length of the binding, sewing the flag shapes inside the binding, and sewing the binding closed at the same time. Remove the pins as you come to them. Iron the entire piece flat.

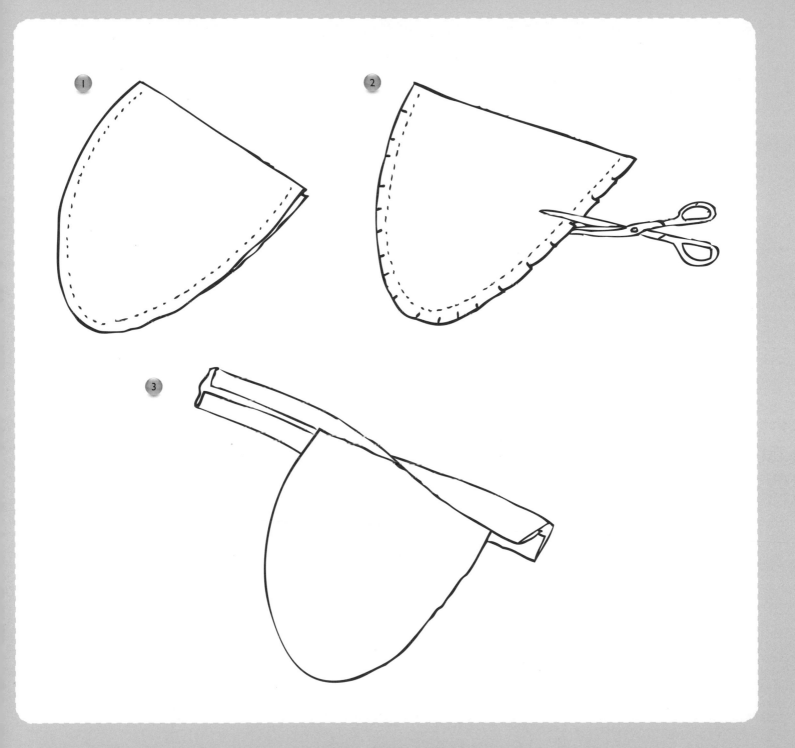

Sweet Embroidered Bird

This little bluebird, perched on a leafy branch, thinks that life is pretty sweet, but the banner she holds in her beak can say anything you like! To customise your hoop, when tracing the pattern, leave the banner space blank and write in your name or your own favourite phrase for greeting the day.

project by: melissa crowe
suitable for: confident beginners
should take: 2–3 hours

SHOPPING LIST

- White or ivory linen (25 cm square)
- Embroidery thread in blue, pink, brown, green, light green, black and deep pink
- Glue
- Wooden embroidery hoop, 15 cm in diameter

CRAFTY NEEDS

- Scissors
- Pinking shears or decorative edge scissors (optional)
- Embroidery needle
- Transfer pencil or carbon paper
- Iron
- Pencil

TEMPLATES

You will need the Sweet Embroidered Bird template for this project.

TECHNIQUES

Hand stitches, page 9

NOTES

- Select your own embroidery colours – red bird? Purple branch? Great!
- Choose another shade of linen or printed cotton. Make sure you select contrasting colours so your design stands out.
- The embroidery hoop will sit on a thumbtack or nail, but you can also string a ribbon through the mechanism at the top.
- If using a transfer pencil, draw or trace your design with the transfer pencil onto paper. Place the paper face down onto the wrong side of your fabric and iron the paper onto your fabric. The heat from the iron will transfer the design onto your fabric.

The fat cat

sweet.

HOW TO MAKE

1. Trace or photocopy the embroidery pattern. Transfer the design onto your fabric using either carbon paper or a special transfer pencil, positioning it in the centre of your fabric.

2. Secure your fabric square in the wooden hoop. To make the fabric wrinkle-free and drum-tight, alternate between pulling the fabric tight and tightening the screw mechanism at the top of your hoop. Do this until there are no more wrinkles in the fabric and the mechanism is turned as far as it will go.

3. Using the photo as your colour guide, stitch over your transferred design using a backstitch. Use all six strands of embroidery floss for everything except the word sweet. For this, use three strands of floss. For each of the bird's eyes, make a teensy '+' with two very small stitches. For her beak, just stitch across the triangle.

4. To finish the back, trim the fabric around the hoop, leaving about 2.5 cm of fabric all the way around. Turn the hoop over so the back faces you. Apply a line of glue to the top of the inside hoop. Carefully fold the fabric over, all the way around, gluing it to the inside hoop. You may need to hold it down for a couple of minutes to allow the fabric to stick firmly. Let the glue dry and then trim off excess fabric — if you have pinking shears or decorative-edge scissors on hand, use them for this step as it looks neater, but regular scissors are just fine.

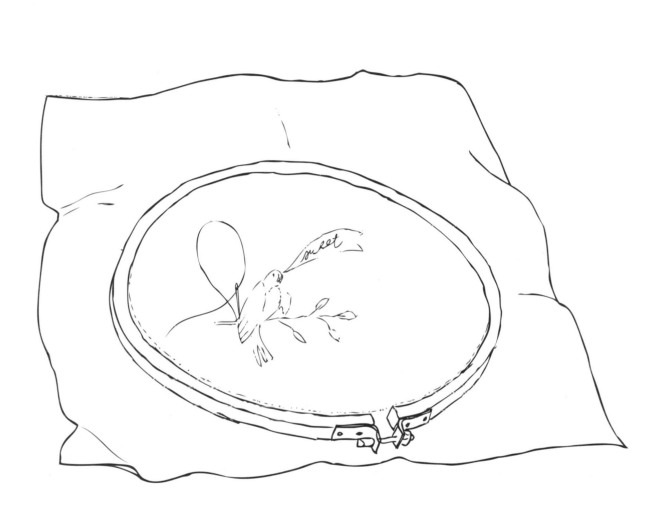

Hanging Art Pouch

This pouch is a creative way to keep art supplies (notebooks, pens, pencils, paintbrushes, rulers, rubber stamps, scissors and so on) nearby and easily accessible. It can hang from a doorknob, a hook, or a bulletin board. A pair of cherries is cross-stitched onto this design, but you might like to stitch your initials or leave out this step altogether.

project by: shannon dréval
suitable for: confident beginners
should take: an afternoon

SHOPPING LIST

- Two contrasting cotton fabrics of your choice (each 18 x 41 cm)
- Sewing thread to match
- Lightweight fusible interfacing (17 x 40 cm)
- String or cord (36 cm)
- A wooden dowel (23 cm)
- Linen for cross stitch (20 x 20 cm)
- Ricrac, 18 cm
- Embroidery thread in red, green and white

CRAFTY NEEDS

- Sewing machine
- Scissors
- Iron
- Embroidery needle
- Embroidery hoop (optional)
- Pins

TECHNIQUES

Hand stitches, page 9

NOTES

- You could use different styles and colours of cotton prints as well as different trims and buttons. Instead of a wooden dowel try a pencil or thin paintbrush to hang the pouch. Instead of string or cord, you could use colourful yarn.
- If you are not doing a cross-stitch design, you can skip the cross-stitch instructions.

HOW TO MAKE

1. Make your cross-stitch design using the chart for the cherry cross stitch. Thread your needle with two strands of embroidery floss. Start stitching in the centre of your linen. On the chart (see diagram 1), each square represents one stitched 'x' and two strands of linen. So for each 'x' (or square on the chart), you'll count two threads of linen over, and two threads of linen up. Then you just stitch the 'x's, from bottom left of the 'x' to top right of the 'x', then back over, from bottom right to top left. All of the 'x's should be stitched in the same direction.

2. For lines for the cherry stems use a backstitch. When cross stitching, rather than making a knot, always finish by threading your needle through three or four threads on the back of your piece. Once finished with your cross stitch, trim your linen so that it measures 5 x 5 cm. Fold under 1.5 cm on all four sides. Press the folds. Place it on the outer piece of fabric, 8 cm down from the seam, 3 cm in from the right-hand edge, and sew it on by hand using a running stitch or whipstitch.

3. Cut out your outer and inner fabrics (18 x 41 cm), your interfacing (17 x 40 cm), string or cord (36 cm) and ricrac (18 cm).

4. Iron the fusible interfacing onto the wrong side of your lining fabric. This will help make your pouch smooth, and it will also give it some structure.

5. Lay this lining fabric right side up and place the outer piece of fabric on top of it, right side down. Pin these together. Only sew one short end then press this seam open.

6. Turn these pieces over so that their wrong sides are facing each other (see diagram 2). Fold on the sewn line then press again. Sew a row of topstitching about 0.5 cm down from, and parallel to, the seam. This will give your pouch a more finished look. Sew a strip of ricrac or other decorative ribbon about 1 cm down from this sewn line.

7. Lay this piece in front of you with the front piece facing up, and the seam at the top. Measure 16 cm down from your topstitched seam and fold under (see diagram 3). Press the fold. Then fold only the outer piece up, in the opposite direction and on the same fold line, so that the outer piece of fabric is now right side of outer fabric to right side of outer fabric. Press the folds and pin together.

8. Sew around the three unfinished edges, leaving a 6 cm opening in the other short end (see diagram 4). Turn right side out using a chopstick or pencil to push out corners and press.

9. With the front of your pouch facing you, measure 2.5 cm down from the top of the pouch and make a fold away from you and toward the back of the pouch. Press the fold. Now, sew this folded piece to

the back of the pouch, with your seam about 5 cm from the edge. While you do this, you'll be sewing the opening closed.

10. Slide the dowel through the top of your pouch and tie the string or cord to each side of the dowel (see diagram 5). Voilà! You're finished!

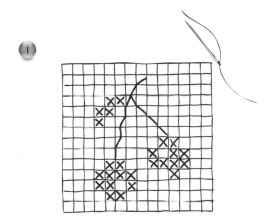

Published in 2011 by Hardie Grant Books

Hardie Grant Books (Australia)
85 High Street
Prahran, Victoria 3181
www.hardiegrant.com.au

Hardie Grant Books (UK)
Second Floor, North Suite
Dudley House
Southampton Street
London WC2E 7HF
www.hardiegrant.co.uk

National Library of Australia Cataloguing-in-Publication Data:
Title: Sewing / edited by Kathreen Ricketson.
ISBN: 9781742700403 (hbk.)
Series: Kids' crafternoon.
Subjects: Sewing.
Other Authors/Contributors: Ricketson, Kathreen.
Dewey Number: 646.2

Publisher: Paul McNally
Project editor: Jane Winning
Design and art direction: Heather Menzies
Photography: Alicia Taylor
Styling: Rachel Vigor
Editing: Catherine Etteridge
Colour reproduction by Splitting Image Colour Studio
Printed in China by 1010 Printing International Limited